I0093300

ANGLOPHOBIA:
The Unrecognised Hatred

Harry Richardson & Frank Salter

Published by Social Technologies in Sydney Australia 2022

www.socialtechnologies.com.au

Via CreateSpace

An earlier version of this book was serialised in *Quadrant* magazine, Australia, in

April, May, June and July-August 2022.

Copyright © Harry Richardson and Frank Salter

First edition 26th January 2023

ISBN Number 978-0-6457163-2-0

All rights reserved. No part of this publication may be reproduced, stored in retrieval system, copied in any form or by any means, electronic, mechanical, photocopying, recording or otherwise transmitted without written permission from the publisher, who can be contacted at harryyo@gmail.com.

The right of Harry Richardson and Frank Salter to be identified as authors of this work has been asserted by them in accordance with sections 77 and 78 of the Copyright, Designs and Patents Act 1988.

Acknowledgment of the
Australian Nation

We acknowledge the Anglo explorers,
pioneers and their descendants
who planted the British flag and
Christian faith on this continent,
creating the Australian nation.

We acknowledge the Aboriginal and
Torres Strait Islander peoples
who have lived here since the Dreamtime.

And we acknowledge the
Federal Commonwealth of Australia,
created by the nation under the Crown to
guard the nation and
the liberty of all citizens.

Harry Richardson is the author of the best-selling *The Story of Mohammed: Islam Unveiled* and editor in chief of *The Richardson Post.*

Frank K. Salter's research areas include the politics of ethnicity. His work has been published by university presses and in reference books on social science. He has published several books including *On Genetic Interests, Welfare, Ethnicity and Altruism* and *The War on Human Nature in Australia's Political Culture.*

CONTENTS

1. Introduction

Being born white is to win the lottery of life. At least that is the conventional wisdom, and in many cases it rings true. White nations, and particularly Anglosphere nations like Australia, are the destination of choice for most of the world's would-be migrants. Their standard of living is the envy of most of the rest of the world. Added to that, they have advanced justice systems, the rule of law, free speech, low levels of corruption, and a welfare system which pays people for simply existing.

Being white in a white nation is a double privilege, we are told. These countries were built by – and for – people like you.

And yet... and yet.

There are things, often small things, which are easy to ignore and assuming that you aren't silly enough to break the unspoken rules, life can go on for the most part without ever really having to think about them too much. There are words you mustn't say, people you mustn't criticise and policies you have to go along with, even if you don't really agree with them.

Occasionally, these "things" can have more tangible effects. These can range from needing a higher score for university entrance to being passed over for a job or a promotion.

For the really unfortunate, however, the reality of the situation can be nothing short of catastrophic.

In the UK, thousands upon thousands of school aged girls were taken as actual sex slaves by gangs of men who were mostly of Pakistani origin. When the parents of these poor wretches reported these monstrous crimes to the police, they were ignored or turned away because, "y'know – racism".

How can it be that the supposedly privileged majority can be treated with such utter contempt by the authorities who have a sworn duty to protect them and claim to do so with an approach that is completely colourblind?

Most of us are instinctively aware of the answer to this conundrum. The reality is, that whilst "racism" is supposedly the greatest evil, the modern definition of racism is not what it appears to be.

Racism is supposed to be discrimination against, or hatred of, people of a particular race or ethnicity. Yet the reality is that there is one race which is not at all protected by the anti-racism zealots. That race is the white race of people who are increasingly discriminated against and defamed. This discrimination is committed by individuals, corporations, governments, media (including the ironically named "social media") and more.

In fact, the majority of the institutions of western nations are increasingly hostile to western interests and act as if the marginalisation of white people and their history and culture would be a good thing.

Why is this? How did it happen? Who, or what were responsible for this disaster and what can we do about it?

One of the major tactics used by the radical left and their minority clients to gain power has been the weaponisation of victimhood. In order to enforce and amplify this advantage, they have adopted, or invented, words to describe any discrimination or injustice against them. These words become powerful weapons when wielded by anti-western radicals. These attack-words have been used without restraint to advance the interests of these groups against the founding majority.

White, and particularly Anglo, culture strongly discourages victimhood. Instead, it encourages self-determination and stoicism, encapsulated in the historic British concept of the "stiff upper lip."

Unfortunately, in the face of organised and well-funded minority victimhood strategies, Anglo stoicism has been a losing response.

Whites need to recognise and identify injustices against them and against their group interests. They need to push back hard against these attacks. In order to do so, they need a word that encapsulates attacks upon them that are, or at least should be, unacceptable to most reasonable people.

The word should not be "clunky". It should roll off the tongue with ease. It also does not need to be strictly accurate. The term "Semite" is not exclusive to Jews, yet we all understand that "anti-Semitism" refers to hostility to Jews.

After casting around and trying various combinations, we arrived, largely by process of elimination, at the term "Anglophobia."

We understand that the term "Anglo" may not resonate with many whites who are affected by this phenomenon. In North America, many may find it jarring due to having non-English ancestors or due to the historic schism with Great Britain. Once the term becomes accepted and slides into the everyday lexicon, however, people will instinctively understand its meaning, even if they themselves might not identify specifically as Anglos.

Once these minor obstacles have receded, the ease of pronunciation make this the clear favourite, one reason why we have chosen it above all possible others such as "white-o-phobia" or the somewhat nihilistic "blank-o-phobia".

The following book is the distillation of example after example of egregious Anglophobic behaviours. Whilst many of these examples occurred in Australia, there is no shortage of equal or greater injustices being perpetrated on an almost daily basis in other traditionally white nations around the world.

This is far from a complete study, but we hope it will inspire an awakening and further research and examination by those who come after us.

2. Why Anglophobia

In recent decades, the taboo against hostile discrimination has intensified. Racism, sexism, homophobia, Islamophobia, anti-Semitism, and trans-phobia have been elevated to a point where they are now considered tantamount to criminal acts.

Yet during the same period, discrimination against Anglos has been largely ignored.

[Note: In this document, the term 'Anglo' refers to people descended from the indigenous population of the British Isles in Australia and overseas as well as those who have assimilated into those populations. It can include kindred ethnic and cultural categories, namely people of European descent and western civilisation as a whole.]

This discrimination needs a name commensurate with its importance. We have chosen the term "Anglophobia". A clear statement of the scope and types of Anglophobia has become necessary.

Anglophobia is defined as hostility towards, aversion to, or discrimination against Anglo people. Anglophobia can be displayed by non-Anglos, by other white ethnicities, and by Anglos themselves. Hostility and suspicion toward Anglo and white Australians have become systemic within multicultural institutions. This hostility appears to be intensifying as ethno-religious diversity increases. It is harming Australians in general and Anglos in particular.

If the other identity phobias are valid concepts for describing hostility towards particular groups, then so too is "Anglophobia".

Anglophobia helps to motivate policies which disadvantage the Anglo majority. These include unrestricted large-scale immigration that is transforming our society. They also include assaults on the Anglo identity of children by the school system. Australians have never been asked to vote for these policies. Instead, they have been imposed by edict.

Multiculturalism is a policy pursued by the governments of Anglosphere nations and many others in the West since the 1970s. The form of multiculturalism adopted is not the advertised normative type. Diversity and ethnic pride are not universally celebrated. Instead, multicultural policies are often aggressive towards the founding ethnic group, acting like a form of cultural warfare intended to defeat Anglos demographically, economically, and psychologically. From its beginnings in the 1970s, Anglo advocates were excluded from multicultural forums and remained the prime targets of multicultural attacks on freedom of speech and association. This is intolerable in a law-governed democracy.

If institutional Anglophobia is to be eliminated, it must first be put under the spotlight, examined, and understood. To that end, we now list some types of Anglophobia. We then devote most of the book to describing these types and providing examples.

3. Types of Anglophobia

A. Vilification

The most common form of Anglophobia is vilification. Anglophobia is the assertion or implication that Anglos in Australia or elsewhere, unlike people of other races or ethnicities:

A. Are inherently evil.
B. Detract from but never enhance diversity.
C. Are responsible for any and all negative actions of members of their race throughout history, because:
  1. They engaged in colonialism which was universally bad.
  2. Are responsible or owe reparations for slavery or other harmful practices carried out by other Anglo or white people before they were born. Therefore they:
  3. Should have their children taught to believe that their own people, history, traditions and culture have transgressed the rights of non-European ethnic groups.
D. Are considered prone to racism according to the ideology of "Critical Race Theory", even when no direct evidence of racism exists. This means that they
  1. Are considered guilty of holding "white supremacist" beliefs for simply expressing

or advocating on behalf of white or Anglo identity.

2. Are uniquely culpable of racism due to their power over non-whites always and everywhere.

3. Must be racist because they are on average wealthier, healthier, or better educated than some other racial or ethnic groups.

E. Must be denied the freedom of speech required to promote or pursue the interests of their group, unlike other racial or ethnic groups, and

1. Should have their free speech right to express ethnic identity regulated by multicultural agencies such as the Human Rights Commission.

2. Should have their expressions of ethnic or cultural pride, solidarity, and identity blocked or removed from media platforms.

F. Must not be allowed a homeland in which they may remain the majority.

G. May have their cultural and religious traditions trivialised, denigrated or eradicated.

B. Hostile Discrimination

Anglo Australians are routinely discriminated against in employment and promotion, despite (or more likely because of) an elaborate system of so-called equal opportunity legislation and accompanying bureaucracies. The Equal Employment Opportunity and Affirmative Action regime is part of the multicultural establishment. It is designed and managed to benefit designated victim groups, which include various ethnic minorities but exclude Anglo identity. Indeed, ethnic affirmative action amounts to jobs and promotions being taken from Anglos and given to others. Another important form of discrimination against Anglos is the use of the education system to indoctrinate school children. Anglo advocates have been ethnically cleansed from this and other institutions, including Big Tech and Big Social Media.

C. Violence

Unsurprisingly, vilification and discrimination are sometimes followed by the most extreme form of Anglophobia. This consists of physical attacks against individuals motivated by hostility towards their Anglo identity. Types of violence include the sexual assault of Anglo women and girls based on their ethnicity. Those who excuse, ignore, trivialise, or cover up these crimes are also culpable.

These points are discussed in more detail presently. Before doing so, however, some general principles and key terms will be defined.

4. Some General Principles

The meaning of "Anglos" has changed over the centuries. The name originates from the Angles, one of the Germanic peoples who settled parts of the British Isles after the Romans evacuated around 450 AD. "Anglo Saxon" became the collective term for those peoples, and also named their language, with the term "Anglo" transforming into "English". In Australia, the root word is retained in the term "Anglo-Celtic", meaning the amalgam of English, Scottish, Welsh and Irish peoples who constituted most of the white population from colonial times. In some countries "Anglo" designates English-speaking white people. Thus, the meaning of "Anglo" has broadened, though perhaps less in the eyes of observers than among Anglos themselves. At the same time the constituent identities remain, especially from the subjective perspective of those in the Old Country. A residue of past disputes remains in the memory of older Australians. Despite this history, the similarity of British-Isles-descended peoples is manifest.

In this document we adopt this broader meaning of "Anglo".

In psychology a phobia is an extreme and involuntary fear reaction, such as fear of heights or of being outdoors. The meaning includes the milder reaction of xenophobia, such as the aversion to strangers that begins at around five months in children. In politics a broader meaning was in use by the early twentieth century, when "Anglophobia" designated hostility towards England or Britain. By late in the twentieth century the suffix "phobia" was being used to designate hostility towards many religious or sexual categories. "Islamophobia", "Judaeophobia", "homo-phobia" and "transphobia" are a few of the more common examples. Applications of the suffix continue to increase.[1]

Perhaps the earliest study of Anglophobia was by James Gwin Cook, an American author who in 1919 wrote a book titled, *Anglophobia: An analysis of anti-British prejudice in the United States*. Cook distinguished types of hostile reaction to Britain, all characterised, he thought, by ignorance or obsession with long dead causes. This included Irish and German dislike of England.[2] (Irish Anglophobia in Australia is discussed in section 5a below.) As early as the War of 1812, American Anglophobia emerged as fantasies about vast English conspiracies,[3] though it was no fantasy when, in that year, the British navy sailed up

---

[1] Greene, A. and M. Mannheim. (2021). Defence declares war on political correctness, bans morning teas aimed at promoting inclusion and diversity, ABC News, 21 May, https://www.abc.net.au/news/2021-05-21/defence-chief-angus-campbell-political-correctness-morning-teas/100156436.

[2] Cook, J. G. (1919). *Anglophobia: An analysis of anti-British prejudice in the United States*. Boston, The Four Seas Company, https://archive.org/details/anglophobiaanan00cookgoog/page/n8/mode/2up, accessed 11.5.2021.

[3] Peskin, L. A. (2011). Conspiratorial Anglophobia and the War of 1812. *The Journal of American History* 98: 647-669.

the Potomac River and burned Congress and the White House to the ground.

Cook's thesis, that dislike of Britain originated in real or imagined conflict, suggests why Anglophobia was widespread a century ago. At its height around 1900, the British Empire ruled almost a quarter of the world's land surface and traded with much of the remainder. This vast enterprise brought subject peoples and many others into contact with Anglo administrators, soldiers, missionaries, traders and, in what would become Anglosphere countries, settlers from Britain.

In the present document, "Anglophobia" names something personal. It is the dislike or mistrust of British-descended people wherever they reside around the world, though mostly in Anglophone countries.[4] The new meaning usually applies within, not between, countries. Also, the word and the sentiments it describes cannot usually be applied to the past. For example, Americans of 1812 could not have been

---

[4] The racism meaning of Anglophobia has been adopted by the British Australian Community (BAC), a community service organisation representing the interests of Anglo Australians. The BAC has for many years been reporting cases of Anglophobic vilification. The following examples come from the society's magazine, *Endeavour*:

Circa 2001. https://endeavour-online.com/2020/08/21/anglophobia-costs-australia-millions/

April/May 2011. https://endeavour-online.com/2020/08/21/anglophobia-7-8-of-australian-residents-hate-brits/

February 2012. https://endeavour-online.com/2020/08/21/another-anglophobe/

June 2012. https://endeavour-online.com/2020/08/21/anglophobic-historians/

Anglophobic in the ethnic sense unless they hated themselves, a phenomenon yet to arrive.

This raises a question. If Cook was correct, then a degree of Anglophobia was understandable, if not excusable, a century ago at the height of the British Empire. It is not a straightforward matter to explain why Anglophobia became more common after the British dismantled their empire, and why it is frequently evident among leftist Anglos within English-speaking societies, which show relatively high levels of openness and tolerance.

Though hostility towards Anglo ethnicity and culture has been increasing since the 1960s, the term "Anglo-phobia" is not in common usage. Neither is it recognised by the multicultural establishment, which does not classify Anglos as a protected group. Most multicultural scholarship treats Anglos as perpetrators, not victims, of prejudice. This is unfair because Anglos have for many years been subjected to vilification on a large scale. Consider the mainstream Australian media.

Over the period 2012-2013 the second author of this paper documented 215 articles and TV programs touching on ethnicity and the national question. These were found in leading Australian newspapers and popular television and radio programs. Topics included Aborigines, refugees, racism, multi-culturalism and diversity, national identity, foreign investment, international relations, and overseas ethnic conflict. Twenty of these articles and programs ethnically defamed Anglos or whites, accusing them of "smugness", "hypocrisy and racism", "fraud", "idiotic" conversation, having a special problem with racism, of detracting from diversity, and in particular of being too numerous in boardrooms, among university faculty, and in television programs, and adhering to offensive commemorations such as Australia Day and Anzac Day. No other ethnicity was defamed.

Many of these accusations came from high status individuals, including a race discrimination commissioner, television personalities, newspaper columnists, a retired judge, Germaine Greer, university professors, Aboriginal leaders, and a serving foreign minister.

The sample also revealed the mainstream media's acceptance of this defamation. No space was provided for counter views. The media were biased and un-self-critical.[5]

Anglophobia continues to trickle and sometimes gush into public culture. Biased news reports, documentaries and commentaries push negative images of white Australians, using prestigious platforms such as SBS Television and the voices of selected academics.[6]

---

[5] Salter, F. K. (2017/2012). Australia and the national question. Part I: The media. *The war on human nature in Australia's political culture. Collected essays I.* Sydney, Social Technologies: 66-87, pp. 73-79. Originally published in *Quadrant*, October 2012: http://www.quadrant.org.au/magazine/issue/2012/10/the-war-against-human-nature-iii-race-and-the-nation-in-the-media

[6] Salter, F. K. (2018). "The inherent racism of SBS's multiculturalism, Part I. A review of the Ray Martin/SBS documentary, *Is Australia Racist?*" *Quadrant* 62(Jan.-Feb.): 58-64, https://quadrant.org.au/magazine/2018/2001-2002/inherent-racism-sbss-multiculturalism/.

Government-mandated school curricula and rituals are systematically Anglophobic, as detailed below.

In our definition of Anglophobia, we recognise that it is one manifestation of psychological propensities that are universal to human beings. We do not maintain that Anglos are purely victims and other groups only perpetrators. We are all humans and therefore capable of aggression and unfairness. Nevertheless, Anglophobia deserves attention because it is common in the media and in the educational system.

In fact, hatred of Anglos is a core feature of multicultural ideology in Anglosphere societies. Anglos are the only ethnicity denied full participation in multicultural politics, because the system was developed in opposition to their interests.[7] Even a simple declaration of Anglo or white identity is liable to be attacked. This is not true for any other ethnic identity.[8]

As already noted, multiculturalism has the appearance of cultural warfare designed to harm Anglos demographically, economically, and psychologically. This ideology and its associated practices should be exposed in plain language and repudiated.

---

[7] Brown, D. (2000). *Contemporary nationalism. Civic, ethnocultural and multicultural politics*. London, Routledge, p. 132.
Kaufmann, E. (2004). *The rise and fall of Anglo-America*. Cambridge, MA, Harvard University Press, p. 193.
[8] Kaufmann, E. (2018). *Whiteshift: Populism, immigration, and the future of white majorities*, Penguin.

5. Psychological & Biological Dimensions of Racism

Since Anglophobia is a form of racism, to understand it necessitates analysing that larger category. Racism can be defined as hostility in thought or deed directed towards individuals or groups by virtue of their ethnic identity. Ethnocentrism, xenophobia and other "groupish" behaviours are not the same as racism, though they share some psychological dimensions. They are all human universals, meaning they are evident in every population that has so far been studied. As explained below, Anglos are among the world's most individualist and least collectivist (in other words, non "racist") cultures. Differences in ethnic behaviours – those predicated on ethnic identity – are quantitative, not qualitative. In other words, all groups show them, though in varying degrees. Research into conduct contingent on social identity has revealed a number of types.

Ethnocentrism. This is a concept invented by the American sociologist William Sumner in 1906.[9] "Loyalty to the group, sacrifice for it, hatred and contempt for outsiders, brotherhood within, warlikeness without—all grow together, common products of the same situation. It is sanctified by connection with

---

[9] Sumner, W. G. (1906). *Folkways*. Boston, Ginn, p. 13.

religion. Men of an others-group are outsiders with whose ancestors the ancestors of the we-group waged war. . . . Each group nourishes its own pride and vanity, boasts itself superior, exalts its own divinities, and looks with contempt on outsiders." Thus, ethnocentrism engenders feelings of superiority or "supremacy", a term too often applied exclusively to white ethnocentrism. Sumner's formulation included xenophobia – hatred and contempt – as an integral part of ethnocentrism. The two behaviours are now seen as distinct, though related. Ethnocentrism is part of a wider range of psychological mechanisms dealing with social identity. These include the propensity of humans to join and identify with groups and to view their own groups positively (ethnocentrism) and other groups negatively (xenophobia).[10] This tendency appears to be innate, the result of biological evolution, because it emerges in childhood, is a cross-cultural universal, and is shown by Man's closest animal relative, chimpanzees.

The evolutionary explanation takes note of the danger posed by tool-using humans. Since humans are apex predators, as their populations grow, neighbouring human groups become an important part of the hostile environment. This human environment selects for the groupish instincts discussed earlier, because humans who have greater group solidarity have an evolutionary advantage over those who do not. Further evidence of innateness comes from the effect of oxytocin on men

[10] Sherif, M. (1966). *In common predicament: The social psychology of intergroup conflict*. Boston, Houghton-Mifflin.

and women. In women, this hormone promotes individual bonding and caring. It is released during breast feeding and sex. In men, oxytocin increases ethnocentrism. Double-blind administration of oxytocin shows that the hormone boosts men's protectiveness towards their group and promotes group trust, cooperation and defensiveness. It does not increase aggression towards competing groups, further evidence that ethnocentrism is distinct from xenophobia.[11] All this is compatible with the theory that humans are evolved to live in groups, identify with and contribute to them, because the welfare of the group affects its members' reproductive fitness.[12]

Xenophobia. Fear and loathing of strangers are closer to the common-sense meaning of racism. Xenophobia is described by part of Sumner's statement, quoted above. It is a universal stage of child development from about five to 10 months.[13] This precedes the emergence of self-identity. Xenophobia is also known

---

[11] de Dreu, C. K. W., L. L. Greer, G. A. V. Kleef, S. Shalvi and M. J. J. Handgraaf (2011). "Oxytocin promotes human ethnocentrism", *Proceedings of the National Academy of Science (US)*.
http://www.pnas.org/content/early/2011/01/06/1015316108, accessed 23.3.2022.
de Dreu, C. K. W., L. L. Greer, M. J. J. Handgraaf, S. Shalvi, G. A. V. Kleef, M. Baas, F. S. T. Velden, E. V. Dijk and S. W. W. Feith (2010). "The neuropeptide oxytocin regulates parochial altruism in intergroup conflict among humans." *Science* 328: 1408-1411.e

[12] MacDonald, K. B. (2001). "An integrative evolutionary perspective on ethnicity." *Politics and the Life Sciences* 20(1): 67-79.

[13] Eibl-Eibesfeldt, I. (1989/1984). *Human ethology*. New York, Aldine de Gruyter, pp. 170-177.

as "negative ethnocentrism". Both xenophobia and ethnocentrism are discriminatory. Xenophobia is discrimination against an individual or group, whilst ethnocentrism is discrimination for. Parenthetically, this makes "discrimination" a socially neutral concept because social engagement entails making discriminations of various kinds. When "discrimination!" is used as an accusation, it is usually short-hand for discrimination *against* an individual or group. Xenophobia can lead to stigmatisation, causing hostility towards a particular identity that can persist in a population for generations. Fear of unfamiliar individuals is opposed by interest in socialising, also a universal of human cultures. Both tendencies were adaptive in the evolutionary past and are shown by other primates. As a result, social contact between strangers is qualified by ambivalence.

Individualism-collectivism. Collectivism is another common-sense element of racism. People belonging to collectivist cultures are more likely than those in individualist cultures to make decisions based on the rules and welfare of their groups. These groups can be families, clans, ethnicities and religions.[14] Collectivism has been measured and compared around the

---

[14] Hoorn, A. v. (2015). "Individualist-collectivist culture and trust radius: A multilevel approach." *Journal of Cross-Cultural Psychology* 46(2): 269-276.

Triandis, H. C. (1972). *The analysis of subjective culture*. New York, Wiley.

Triandis, H. C. et al. (1986). "The measurement of the etic aspects of individualism and collectivism across cultures." *Australian Journal of Psychology* 38(No. 3): 257-267.

world, notably by social psychologist Harry Triandis.[15] People who score highly on collectivism will often override their personal preferences in order to serve their kinship group. Collectivist cultural regions include North Africa, the Middle East, and China. By contrast, Anglos bear the culture that evolved in North-Western Europe, one of the most individualist cultural regions. The social psychologist Richard Nisbett has found that this cultural dimension affects ways of thinking. Westerners have tunnel vision, while East Asians are more holistic. Westerners are more prone to believe they can understand and therefore manipulate things, Asians less so. The two cognitive styles coincide with western individualism and Asian collectivism.[16]

Assortment by similarity. Racism is also thought to consist of preference for one's own ethnic group, though this is a prosocial form of ethnocentrism unlike antisocial xenophobia. The old adage, "Birds of a feather flock together" has been well confirmed for humans. Most people prefer to marry, live among and work with their own ethnic group.[17] This is often true of individuals whose conscious political values run in the opposite direction, that is, who praise diversity.

---

[15] Triandis, H. C. et al. (1986). "The measurement of the etic aspects of individualism and collectivism across cultures", *op cit.*

[16] Nisbett, R. (2004). *The geography of thought: How Asians and Westerners think differently . . . and why*, Free Press.

[17] McPherson, M., L. Smith-Lovin and J. M. Cook (2001). Birds of a feather: Homophily in social networks. *Annual Review of Sociology*. K. S. Cook and J. Hagan. Palo Alto, California, Annual Review. 27: 415-444.

The result is that diverse societies are prone to sort themselves by ethnicity as well as by income and ideology. The United States today is as segregated – voluntarily – as it was during the height of forced segregation a century ago.[18] Ethnic assortment is not surprising when it is realised that ethnic groups are pools of genetic kinship.[19]

Ethnic group interests. Relations between ethnic groups can become fraught and sometimes savage because those groups carry vital interests for their members. As early as the 1970s the evolutionary biologist William Hamilton suggested that ethnicities are large pools of genetic kinship and that it is adaptive for their members to care for their ethnic groups.[20] This is because ethnicity is defined as descent from common ancestors. Ethnic kinship was quantified in 2002 by geneticist Henry Harpending in conjunction with political ethologist Frank Salter.[21] An ethnic

---

[18] Bishop, B. (2009). *The big sort: Why the clustering of like-minded America is tearing us apart*. Boston, Mariner Books.

[19] Harpending, H. (2002). "Kinship and population subdivision." *Population and Environment* 24(2): 141-147.

Salter, F. K. (2007/2003). *On genetic interests: Family, ethnicity, and humanity in an age of mass migration*. New Brunswick, N.J., Transaction Publishers.

[20] Hamilton, W. D. (1971). Selection of selfish and altruistic behavior in some extreme models. Man and beast: Comparative social behavior. J. F. Eisenberg and W. S. Dillon. Washington, D.C., Smithsonian Institute Press: 59-91, Appendix B.

[21] Harpending, H. (2002). "Kinship and population subdivision." *Population and Environment* 24(2): 141-147.

group carries many more copies of its members' gene variants than does the largest family.[22] Ethnic groups also carry cultural and religious interests. Other ethnic interests are social inclusion and cohesion, because as ethno-religious diversity increases, cohesion falls and conflict rises. Most people choose to live among their own people and to make friends and marry among them. Ethnic identity is adaptive because it allows people to defend their ethnic cultural and genetic interests. Conversely, encouraging an ethnic group to lose its identity is like encouraging parents to forget who their children are.

Structural, institutional, and systemic racism. These terms are often used when evidence of actual racism is thin but is nevertheless suspected, for example due to the underrepresentation of protected groups in an organisation or vocation. These types of racism are held to be embedded in the structures and systems of society or organisations. A popular example on the left is the Apartheid regime in South Africa, from 1948 until the early 1990s. Blacks were denied equal rights to whites, for example by being segregated in housing and use of public facilities, and expected to live in their designated tribal homelands. They had to carry a pass to enter white areas. The structural or systemic effect of this contributed to black

---

Salter, F. K. (2002). "Estimating ethnic genetic interests: Is it adaptive to resist replacement migration?" *Population and Environment* 24(2): 111-140.

[22] Salter, F. K. (2007/2003). *On genetic interests: Family, ethnicity, and humanity in an age of mass migration*. New Brunswick, N.J., Transaction Publishers. Harpending's 2002 paper is an appendix.

disadvantage. Harm to blacks did not come only from racist whites but from unjust laws and regulations acting through bureaucracies. Another example of systemic racism is China's policy of cultural genocide directed at Tibetan and Uyghur peoples. The main harm comes not from individual behaviour of the Han majority, but from government policy exercised by the military, police and other bureaucracies.

6. Sociological Dimensions of Racism

Given all the psychological mechanisms underpinning racism, mechanisms that are present in every group of humans, it should be expected that diversity hurts societies that embrace it. It does. Extensive research findings made since the 1970s indicate that ethno-religious diversity imposes substantial social and economic costs. These include ethnic conflict some-times leading to civil war, loss of public trust and cooperation, reduced democracy, reduced economic growth, the emergence of ethnic criminal gangs, and psychological and social harm done to majorities who become minorities.[23]

---

[23] Salter, F. K. (2002). *Risky transactions: Trust, kinship, and ethnicity*. New York, Berghahn Books.

Salter, F. K., Ed. (2004). *Welfare, ethnicity, & altruism: New data & evolutionary theory*. London, Frank Cass.

Vanhanen, T. (2012). *Ethnic conflicts: Their biological roots in ethnic nepotism*. London, Ulster Institute for Social Research.

American diversity effects:

Putnam, R. D. (2007). E Pluribus Unum: Diversity and community in the twenty-first century. The 2006 Johan Skytte Prize lecture. *Scandinavian Political Studies* 30: 137-174.

Australian diversity effects:

Wickes, R., R. Zahnow, G. White and L. Mazerolle (2014). "Ethnic diversity and its impact on community social

Individuals motivated by Anglophobia often accuse Anglos of initiating ethnic conflict. However, none of the above research blames any ethnic group in particular for causing conflict. It is human nature that is the cause, because humans have evolved to survive and prosper in groups which often have conflicting interests.

When discussing ethnic affairs, it is also important to understand how scholars define key concepts. These terms are often conflated by the popular media in their rush to condemn Anglos and white civilisation in general. The following definitions are drawn from the interdisciplinary school of nationalism studies and from biology.[24]

---

cohesion and neighborly exchange." *Journal of Urban Affairs* 36(1): 51-78.

British diversity effects:

Laurence, J. and L. Bentley (2015). "Does ethnic diversity have a negative effect on attitudes towards the community? A longitudinal analysis of the causal claims within the ethnic diversity and social cohesion debate." *European Sociological Review* http://esr.oxfordjournals.org/content/early/2015/08/20/esr.jcv081, accessed 12.5.2021.

Review of this literature:

Salter, F. K. (2018). The biosocial study of ethnicity. *The Oxford handbook of evolution, biology, and society*. R. L. Hopcroft. New York, Oxford University Press: 543-568.

[24] The interdisciplinary school of nationalism studies is organized by the Association for the Study of Ethnicity and Nationalism, founded by Anthony D. Smith. Key publications by Smith, Connor and van den Berghe are cited in subsequent endnotes. Key texts in biology are:

Eibl-Eibesfeldt, I. (1989/1984). *Human ethology*. New York, Aldine de Gruyter.

Ethnic group. This is a named population whose members claim descent from common ancestors, share memories of the same homeland, show normative endogamy (as a rule marry within the group), share some aspects of culture, and show broad solidarity.[25] Ethnic groups are identified by markers that distinguish them from their neighbours. These include such features as language, homeland, religion, style of clothing, ritual scars, and distinctive artefacts, such as style of arrow heads. As Europeans explored the world, they encountered ethnic groups belonging to different races, and race became one common ethnic marker in multi-racial societies. Unlike cultural similarity, racial resemblance is direct evidence of ancestry because it is coded in the genes.

Race. This is a regional or continental-scale population with characteristics evolved in response to local environmental challenges, especially climate and ecology. Visual racial differences are important ethnic markers in mixed-race societies.[26]

Cavalli-Sforza, L. L., P. Menozzi and A. Piazza (1994). *The history and geography of human genes*. Princeton, New Jersey, Princeton University Press.

[25] Smith, A. D. (1986). *The ethnic origins of nations*. Oxford, Basil Blackwell.

[26] Berghe, P. L. v. d. (1981). *The ethnic phenomenon*. New York, Elsevier.

Salter, F. K. and H. Harpending (2013). "J. P. Rushton's theory of ethnic nepotism." *Personality and Individual Differences,* 55: 256-260.
http://www.sciencedirect.com/science/article/pii/S01918869 12005569

Nation. This is an ethnic group living in its homeland. National identity and the resulting bond of nationhood can be maintained as diversity increases, but only if a large ethnic core is maintained. Other components of a nation include a history of communication and trade within that territory.[27] Nationalism is a powerful social and political force. In its modern form it was adopted across Europe and the Anglosphere in the nineteenth century, before spreading around the world. Empires that have fragmented into nations include the Austro-Hungarian, the Ottoman, the British, Dutch, French, Spanish, and the Soviet Union in the early 1990s. Ruling elites seeking legitimacy typically do so by claiming to represent the nation. Nationalism increases the aspiration to be ruled by members of one's own ethnicity. This means that ethnic stratification, now common in western societies, tends to produce social conflict and the growth of countervailing government power.[28]

State. This is a set of governmental organisations that monopolise the use of legitimate violence within a demarcated territory. The first states were kingdoms, city states, and empires. States are usually multi-ethnic.[29] Nation states became popular after the French Revolution, initially in Europe. In Australia, the national state is the Commonwealth, established in

---

[27] Smith, *Ethnic origins*.

[28] Muller, J. Z. (2008). Us and them: The enduring power of
ethnic nationalism. *Foreign Affairs* (March/April).

[29] Connor, W. (1978). A nation is a nation, is a state, is an ethnic
group, is a . . . *Ethnic and Racial Studies* 1(4): 378-400.

1901 from the union of six colonies that are now called "states". This resembles the American model.

Nation State. This is a type of state developed by a nation. In the Old World the borders and names of states typically corresponded to the borders and names of the founding nation. In settler societies such as Australia, the United States of America, and New Zealand, the name of the state is drawn from European names for those territories, not from the ethnic name of the settlers. Nevertheless, they all developed as nation states with unambiguous ethnic identities and origins. Most nation states developed after the French Revolution, but there were early examples in the ancient world, such as Israel and, in the first millennium AD, Armenia and England.[30]

Nationalism exerts centrifugal force on empires by empowering national liberation movements. Most nation states have some degree of ethnic diversity, but have a core identity drawn from the founding ethnicity.[31] Founding ethnic groups naturally feel entitled to control the state apparatus. Nation states that break away from empires benefit from higher trust among citizens, greater political stability, higher economic growth, more democracy, lower corruption and also more generous welfare.[32] These states, which are typically more homogeneous than empires, also have lower ethnic conflict and are much less likely to

---

[30] Smith, A. D. (2004). *The antiquity of nations*, Cambridge Polity.

[31] Smith, *Ethnic origins of nations.*

[32] Alesina, A. and E. Spolaore (2003). *The size of nations*. Cambridge, MA, MIT Press.

be burdened with ethnic political parties, race relations boards, or civil wars.[33] These benefits, together with control of the state and the resulting control of immigration and cultural policy, are of existential importance to the founding ethnic group. Any attempt to wrest control of the state from the founding ethnicity is an aggressive act that strikes at the foundations of its independence and continuity.

The reason empires have broken up into nations is that nationalism's primal political motivation is the desire for sovereignty, meaning self-rule. Thus a universal feature of nationalism is the desire of a people for their own state. Connected with this is the universal rejection of foreign interference in the operation of the nation state.

This definition of nationalism is mainstream. It is accepted by many international relations experts, such as Professor John Mearsheimer of Chicago University.[34] The Professor points out that nationalism is one of the strongest political forces at the global level. The world today consists of almost 200 states each with its own national identity.

---

[33] Calwell, A. A. (1978/1972). *Be just and fear not*. Adelaide, Rigby, p. 118.

Vanhanen, T. (2012). *Ethnic conflicts: Their biological roots in ethnic nepotism*. London, Ulster Institute for Social Research.

[34] John Mearsheimer (2019. The great delusion: Liberal dreams and international realities, speech delivered at the University of London, 21 January 2019.
https://www.youtube.com/watch?v=ni9rncx8ceA&t=928, accessed 14.2.2022.

An example provided by Mearsheimer to illustrate the force and character of nationalism is the Jewish variety, known as Zionism. The founding document for the movement was written by Theodore Herzl in 1896. It was entitled *The Jewish State.* Half a century later, this state was achieved. A mass movement among the Jewish people gained them their own state, thus providing self-rule. Israel is a liberal democracy that protects the rights of citizens of every background. Notably, however, it protects the collective rights only of Jewish citizens.

This analysis of nationalism – that people around the world wish to be ruled by members of their nation – implies that they also wish their elites to share the nation's identity. It also implies that founding nations want to remain a super-majority within their state borders.

We shall now discuss examples of the types of Anglophobia listed in the summary.

7. Examining Types of Anglophobia: *Vilification*

> "[T]here must be something terribly wrong with
> western white civilization. ... The white
> race *is* the cancer of human history;"
>
> Susan Sontag[35]

Vilification comes in many forms. Anglophobic vilification asserts or implies that Australians or others of British-Isles descent, unlike people of other races or ethnicities:

A. Are inherently evil.

No other racial group is maligned in Australia or other Anglophone countries the way that Anglos, and white people in general, are. Actions such as the stereotyping or racial profiling of non-white people are currently considered to be unacceptable in western societies. Meanwhile, the same people who promote this view often insist that all white people are responsible for every sin committed by their ethnic kin. In Australia the negative portrayal of Anglo Australians and the

---

[35] Sontag, S. (1967). What's happening to America? (A Symposium)". *Partisan Review*, 34(1): 57–58.

nation they created entered the school curriculum long ago.[36] The media excuse verbal abuse of Anglos, as if it is understood that whites are contemptible.

Noel Pearson is a Queensland Aboriginal leader who is popular with the multicultural establishment. He has a reputation for crude Anglophobia. For example, in 2012 he was reported accusing government officials and a female journalist, to their faces, of being "f**king racist white c***s".[37] Some commentators took exception to the crudity, but not the racism. Marcia Langton, who is professor of indigenous studies at Melbourne University, sprang to Pearson's defence by explaining that harsh epithets are a normal part of Aboriginal English, serving as "exclamation marks". In the same comment she demonstrated the Anglophobic component of her thesis by sneering at "[t]he Anglo preference for supercilious politeness". The comment was published without apology by the Weekend Australian.[38]

One of the most pernicious examples of Anglophobia came in 1993 from Colin Tatz (1934-2019). He was professor of politics at the University of New England. Tatz, himself an immigrant, was part of the campaign to criminalise "racist" speech. He began by rejecting

---

[36] In the NSW curriculum, examples of racism are limited to Anglos and other whites persecuting other ethnicities. https://www.education.nsw.gov.au/teaching-and-learning/curriculum/multicultural-education/anti-racism-education/countering-racism, accessed 7.5.2021.

[37] Tony Koch, "Pearson yet to learn lessons of leadership", *Weekend Australian*, 28-29 April, Inquirer, p. 18.

[38] Marcia Langton, "Why I continue to be inspired by Pearson", *Weekend Australian*, 5-6 May 2012, Inquirer, p. 20.

the "(often) absurd screech about free speech". He then revealed his underlying motive to be a condemnatory attitude towards the ethnic views and history of Australians. "[W]e are fundamentally a racist society, with an appalling history that includes genocide. We are not wholly convinced about the rhetoric of rights, equality, distributive justice, and fairness. Perhaps, consciously or subconsciously, we want to preserve the right to not only feel what we feel about Aborigines but then to act on such feelings, legitimately."[39] Presumably when Tatz attributed this vileness to "we", he was not genuinely pleading guilty or identifying with the nation. He was blaming others, the masses, the Anglo Australians.

Cultural Marxist vilification of white Australia has often come from institutions captured by the radical left. For example, in 1981 a team from the Soviet-penetrated World Council of Churches[40] spent two weeks visiting Aborigines before pronouncing as fact that "Social Darwinism" had become "grafted into white culture". They claimed that the ideology showed its racist potential when Europeans encountered native peoples. Racist social Darwinism, according to their

---

[39] Tatz, Colin (1993). Racism and rules. *Polemic* 4(2): 79-82, p. 82.
http://www.austlii.edu.au/au/journals/PolemicUSyd/1993/1922.pdf, accessed 24,11,2021.
[40] Metodiev, M. (2010). *Between faith and compromise*. Sofia, Bulgaria, Institute for Studies of the Recent Past. See English language review by Ivaylo Znepolski, https://hssfoundation.org/en/momchil-metodiev-between-faith-and-compromise/, accessed 25.11.2021.

report, is part of white culture.[41] This Anglophobia was sponsored by the Australian Council of Churches, which was networked with the leadership of Australian Protestant denominations. Marxist dogma concerning social Darwinism has become a staple of anti-white vilification, and is generally fallacious or overstated. In the present example, it is difficult to see how Darwin's *Origin of Species,* published in 1859, could have influenced colonial attitudes for the preceding seven decades of settlement, beginning in 1788.

Vilification of white people as evil has reached epidemic proportions in the United States. *The New York Times*, perhaps the most influential newspaper in that country, supports the 1619 Project, which defames Anglo Americans. The author of the Project is Nikole Hannah-Jones, an African-American journalist who once declared that: "[T]he white race is the biggest murderer, rapist, pillager, and thief of the modern world." Furthermore, she claimed that Europeans committed "acts of devils", that they were "barbaric devils", and that Columbus was no different than Hitler. Her reference was not simply to the white people who settled America in the 17th and 18th centuries. She added that "[t]he descendants of these savage [white] people pump drugs and guns into the Black community, pack Black people into the squalor of segregated urban ghettos and continue to be bloodsuckers in our community". Hannah-Jones

---

[41] Adler, Elizabeth, A. Barkat, B. Silu, Q. Duncan and P. Webb (1981). *Justice for Aboriginal Australians: Report of the World Council of Churches team visit to the Aborigines June 15 to July 3, 1981.* Sydney, Australian Council of Churches, 10 August, 91 pp, p. 8.

received the coveted Pulitzer Prize for her work on the 1619 Project.[42]

Anglophobia is sponsored not only by Big Media but by the universities and elements of the corporate world. For example, in a case of institutional Anglophobia in the US in 2021, Coca-Cola required its trainees to complete online lessons in how to "try to be less white". The lesson taught that whites are oppressive, arrogant, defensive, ignorant, apathetic, and racist.[43] A similar lesson has been scripted into some movies produced in recent decades, including the *Matrix* trilogy (1999-2003) in which all of the villains but few of the goodies are Anglo-white men.[44] The

---

[42] Boyd, J. (2020). In racist screed, NYT's 1619 Project founder calls 'white race' 'barbaric devils,' 'bloodsuckers,' Columbus 'No Different Than Hitler', *The Federalist*, 25 June, https://thefederalist.com/2020/06/25/in-racist-screed-nyts-1619-project-founder-calls-white-race-barbaric-devils-bloodsuckers-no-different-than-hitler/, accessed 12.11.2022.

[43] Gioino, C. (2021). 'Blatant discrimination'. Coca-Cola racism training 'asks staff to "try to be less white" as they claim "kids are taught being white is better"'. *The U.S. Sun*. 21 Feb. https://www.the-sun.com/news/2379531/coca-cola-racism-training-staff-to-be-less-white/, accessed 22.2.2021.

[44] Further examples of the "evil white" message are:

Joyce, F. (2015). White men must be stopped: The very future of mankind depends on it. *Salon.com*. 22 December, https://www.salon.com/2015/12/22/white_men_must_be_stopped_the_very_future_of_the_planet_depends_on_it_partner/, accessed 4.5.2021.

Powers, Kirsten (2020). America's overdue reckoning with white supremacy: 'We have allowed evil to flourish', https://www.usatoday.com/story/opinion/voices/2020/06/04/george-floyd-white-supremacy-reparations-column/3135256001/, accessed 4.5.2021.

latter included the Architect of the matrix and all of the police and evil "agents" who persecuted dissenters.

In all these cases, hatred of Anglos is expressed by powerful individuals and institutions. It is an elite project. A virulent form of Anglophobia is Critical Race Theory, discussed in sections 4 and 5 below. It should be noted that this theory often amounts to the dog-whistle accusation of evil aimed exclusively at white people. A recent example is provided by Dr. Donald Moss, a psychoanalyst from New York, who states in a peer-reviewed academic article (in the prestigious *Journal of the American Psychoanalytic Association*) that whiteness is a "malignant, parasitic-like condition to which 'white' people have a particular susceptibility". Citing Sigmund Freud as a source, Moss further maintained that "Parasitic Whiteness" is "almost impossible to eliminate", and "renders its hosts' appetites voracious, insatiable, and perverse". And of course, whiteness is held to disadvantage non-whites.[45]

---

[45] Moss, D. (2021). "On having whiteness." *Journal of the American Psychoanalytic Association* 69(2): 355-371, https://journals.sagepub.com/doi/full/310.1177/000306512110085 07, accessed 5.8.2021.

B. Detract from but never enhance diversity

Government departments, universities, and corporations commonly set "diversity targets". Diversity has an objective meaning, measured by variables such as ethno-cultural heterogeneity and gender ratios. However, an ideological meaning of "diversity" is used increasingly by leftist and multicultural advocates. They speak of the "diversity component" or of people with "diverse backgrounds". This really means non-white or non-male or non-Christian, as if these identities are not real and legitimate. This form of Anglophobia has been around for decades. In 2012 *Sydney Morning Herald* education editor Andrew Stevenson claimed in a front-page article that private schools were insufficiently diverse. The headline contained a racial slur which indicated that insufficiently diverse meant too white. It read: "The white bread playground: top private schools shun ethnic diversity".[46]

The optimum level of diversity is rarely stated. Instead, it is assumed that diversity – meaning people who are not white – is good, and more is always better, which contradicts the research findings reported earlier about the costs of diversity. When corporations or government departments set diversity quotas, they really mean targets that reduce the number of Anglos, whites, males, Christians, or cis-gendered heterosexuals. White society and only white society is

---

[46] Andrew Stevenson, *Sydney Morning Herald*, 12 June 2012, p. 1. https://www.smh.com.au/education/the-white-bread-playground-top-private-schools-shun-ethnic-diversity-20120611-20663.html, accessed 28.12.2022.

accused of lacking diversity and its whiteness is taken as evidence of racism. Other communities, congregated in particular suburbs or nations, do not lack diversity. They *are* diversity, no matter how numerous or geographically concentrated.

The same principle is applied to social niches, such as art museums. The new director of Sydney's Museum of Contemporary Art, Suzanne Cotter, stated that white male artists were not interesting. "It doesn't mean to say you're not a great artist." It is being white and male that's the problem, it "isn't what is relevant for people now. You have to think in a timely way."[47] Cotter also observed that art museums around the world were trying to change the demographic of displayed artists from what she described as a skew towards white men. In her view, diversity in art requires reducing the number of white male artists whose work is shown in galleries.

Media-approved Aboriginal advocates accuse Anglo Australia of being a "white Australian racist monoculture"[48] and Anglo-Australians will always be "settler colonials" no matter how many generations

---

[47] Westwood, M. (2022). White, male artists on notice: you're boring. *The Weekend Australian*. Sydney, News Corp, p. 3, https://www.theaustralian.com.au/arts/visual-arts/white-male-artists-on-notice-youre-boring-says-new-mca-director-suzanne-cotter/news-story/8c90ea85c761e27af7a70fd0c4a0f50b.

[48] Grieve-Williams, Victoria (2021). Proud hunter-gatherers, *The Weekend Australian Review*, 3 July, pp. 14-15. Republished on 5 July 2021 as "Dark Emu 'hoax': takedown reveals the emperor has no clothes", https://www.theaustralian.com.au/arts/review/dark-emu-hoax-takedown-reveals-the-emperor-has-no-clothes/news-story/72525615af286ba3820a0ba95a86095d

they have been in the country.[49] Multicultural activists have accused the Federal Parliament – elected by citizens of all backgrounds – of being too Anglo and in need of more diversity. In 2012 columnist George Megalogenis decried the Federal Parliament's lack of diversity: "It has become more monochrome at the very moment we need to pursue more openness – in markets and in immigration."[50] No mention was made of relatively homogeneous countries such as Japan and China that trade with the world without opening their immigration doors or diversifying their governments.

---

[49] Grieve-Williams, V. (2021). The act of race-shifting, *The Weekend Australian* p. 16.
https://www.theaustralian.com.au/inquirer/its-cultural-fraud-the-act-of-raceshifting/news-story/0e2d97e1a745957a6b36029a9f04f0cb, accessed 14.7.2021.

[50] George Megalogenis, "Reform blues stem from parliament's monochrome demography", *Weekend Australian*, 21-22 July 2012, Inquirer, p. 22.

C. Are responsible for any and all negative actions of members of their race throughout history.

To blame the Chinese community in Australia for the practice of opium dens during the nineteenth century gold rush or for China's appalling treatment of the Tibetans or the Uighurs, would be considered unacceptably racist in this country. Yet Anglos in Australia and overseas are sometimes held responsible for all negative aspects of white behaviour, whilst positive accomplishments are rarely mentioned. Our children are taught little in school about the history of their people. What they do learn is too often taught through a lens of ethnic self-loathing which is not applied to any other people or cultures. In 2012 then Foreign Minister Bob Carr criticised the Opposition leader, Tony Abbott's, statement that Australia is part of the Anglosphere. He linked the statement to what he portrayed as the anti-Asian immigration views of One Nation founder Pauline Hanson in the 1990s. "With our heritage of White Australia and membership of the British Empire . . . it's too risky for us even to glance in the direction of talk of an Anglosphere. It revives all those unfortunate recollections and associations."[51] Carr was, in effect, alleging group guilt. He was judging present-day Australians for the supposed sins committed by other Anglos in the past. This included a common variant of group guilt Anglophobia, the assumption that:

---

[51] Carr takes Abbott to task on Anglo outlook, *Weekend Australian*, 28-29 July 2012, The Nation, p. 6.

C-1. They engaged in colonialism which was universally bad.

Numerous societies throughout history have engaged in conquest and colonisation of other lands. Examples include the colonies of Ancient Greece, the Roman Empire, Han Chinese imperialism, the Muslim invasions of North Africa, the Iberian Peninsula, and the Indian subcontinent, and the colonies of the Polynesians and Torres Strait Islanders. Yet when the word "colonialism" is used in academia, the media, government, or other major institutions, it is presented as abnormal and peculiarly European, especially when carried out by the British. Naturally, the experience of being conquered or colonised has invidious aspects. At the same time, it is often viewed by the colonisers as enterprising and even heroic.

No colonialism has been more remarkable in its achievement than small European countries establishing working societies in lands oceans away. Britain's establishment of thriving colonies in North America and Australasia was an achievement of historic importance. Furthermore, western, especially Anglo, nations bestowed significant benefits on the peoples they colonised. These included systems of constitutional governance, principles such as free speech and the rule of law, English Common Law, the ending of practices such as slavery and *suttee* (the burning of widows in pre-colonial India on the funeral pyres of their husbands), the material and cultural wealth of industry and science, and the western canon of art, literature, music and architecture. Despite these redeeming features, western colonialism is falsely portrayed as failing to provide any benefit at all to those who experienced it. In contrast, non-western colonisers such as the Ottomans, Moors or Chinese, are ignored or given mostly favourable coverage for their artistic, literary, musical, and architectural contributions. A double standard is evident, in which replacement-level immigration to western societies is praised for benefiting the migrants, but historical western colonialism is condemned without reference to its manifold benefits to the immigrants from Europe. This one-sided approach to colonialism as "European bad but all others good" is another case of ingrained and institutionalised Anglophobia.

Anti-colonial sentiment is now being expressed in "cancel culture". In Australia and overseas, statues commemorating white explorers, and political and military leaders have been desecrated or torn down. Attempts are being made to ethnically cleanse whites from the language by changing the names of inventions and scientific discoveries if the inventor or discoverer was white or guilty of a colonial-type sentiment. Thus, efforts are under-way to rename Newton's Laws of Motion the "three fundamental laws of physics" in order to "decentre whiteness" and "decolonise the curriculum".[52]

This push by hostile elites to de-legitimise colonialism, or rather the interests of the descendants of colonists, coincided with some Anglos seeking to remove

---

[52] For references see Krylov, A. I. (2021). The peril of politicizing science. *Journal of Physical Chemistry Letters* 12(22): 5371-5376, https://pubs.acs.org/doi/5310.1021/acs.jpclett.5371c01475, accessed 14.6.2021, endnotes 10, 12, 15, and 35.

restrictions on non-white immigration. During the 1950s and 1960s rejection of colonialism appears to have been an important rationale.

An early example was the Australian poet Alec Derwent Hope (1907–2000), who was educated at Sydney and Oxford universities. In 1939 Hope published a poem titled "Australia". Though the poem contains lines of affection for his country, Hope also expressed anxiety about national inferiority.

> Without songs, architecture, history … …
> And her five cities, like five teeming sores
> Each drains her: a vast parasite robber-state
> Where second-hand Europeans pullulate
> Timidly on the edge of alien shores.

There were several glaring errors in Hope's critique, the least important of which was that by 1939 Australia had six, not five, capital cities. These included one sitting astride the river that shares Hope's middle name. Already, a century earlier, indeed from 1788, Australia shared the ancient history and culture of its mother country. Another error of the poem is to imply that Anglo Australia was somehow parasitic, when in fact the farms and roads and cities were built by the sweat of settlers, many of them ex-convicts. What does it mean to be "second-hand" Europeans? Used? That is meaningless, except for its pejorative connotations. The same applied to "pullulate", which means "to swarm". As for "timidly on the edge", by 1939 Australia was one of the wealthiest and most dynamic economies due not only to its industrialism and integration in the British global trading system, but to the early pioneering farmers and graziers who had ventured inland and made a harsh continent yield riches.

A less poetic but more serious Anglophobic movement only began in the 1950s and 1960s when anti-colonialism became fashionable among intellectuals. In the vanguard was the Immigration Reform Group (IRG), established by leftist Anglo academics in the late 1950s. In 1975 Kenneth Rivett, a lecturer in economics at the University of NSW and leading member of the Group, named the IRG members as himself, Christine Inglis, a lecturer in education at the University of Sydney, Fiona Mackie, a tutor in sociology at La Trobe University, Audrey Rennison, a lecturer in social work at the University of NSW, Alan Ward, a lecturer in history at La Trobe University, and five individuals whose occupations were not listed – R. J. Beveridge, John Darbyshire, K. A. Faulkes, J. A. C. Mackie, and Cyril Manuel.[53]

The Group continued what had become a British intellectual tradition of excessive self-criticism, an expression of a European tendency towards individualism and muted tribalism.[54]

An early pamphlet by the IRG was published in 1960, *Control or Colour Bar?*[55] Let us be clear what the

---

[53] Rivett, K. (1975). *Australia and the non-white migrant*. Melbourne, Melbourne University Press.

[54] MacDonald, K. B. (2019). *Individualism and the Western liberal tradition*. USA, Kindle.

[55] Immigration Reform Group (1962). *Immigration: Control or colour bar? A proposal for change in Australia's immigration policy*. Parts of the pamphlet can be viewed at: https://www.naa.gov.au/learn/learning-resources/learning-

Group's aims were. They wanted to remove the restrictive immigration policy that had shaped the nation into a cohesive, largely homogeneous one. The 1960 version of the Liberal immigration platform, which resembled Labor's had as its 129th policy:

> Preservation of our national heritage by special encouragement and assistance to persons of British stock desiring to settle in Australia.[56]

The Group's pamphlet advanced two reasons why Australia should abandon its traditional immigration policy.

Firstly, it claimed that ethnically selective immigration has bad effects within Australia. It claimed that the policy poisoned race relations and depressed Australia's culture below what it could gain by a small intake of Asians. "We need [Asian immigrants] to enrich our culture." It asserted that an Asian intake would increase Australia's understanding of neighbouring countries, that it would prepare us to participate in racially diverse international forums, and finally, and rather patronisingly, it claimed that breaking down Australia's Anglo homogeneity would make it more effective at helping Asian countries. Significantly, the authors did not urge Asian and African countries to open their borders to whites in order to enrich their cultures and learn how to handle

---

resource-themes/society-and-culture/migration-and-multiculturalism/promoting-migration-reform-pamphlet-control-or-colour-bar, accessed 24.2.2022.

[56] Liberal Party of Australia (1960). *Official federal platform of the Liberal Party of Australia,* approved by the Federal Council, November.

diversity. Perhaps they did not do so because such a message would have sounded like neo-colonialism and racial chauvinism. The double standard was clearly Anglophobic.

The IRG's second reason for urging Asian immigration was to rescue Australia from its racist image overseas. It claimed that the pro-white policy had "a disastrous impact on non-European opinion", because non-whites found the policy "deeply offensive" (p. 11). To universalise this proposition is to falsify it. To have any moral force, it must imply that people around the world find it deeply offensive when other countries do not accept them as immigrants, even when they themselves discriminate in selecting immigrants. It is a fact that Japan fiercely criticised Australia's exclusion of Asians, despite not accepting immigrants itself, and later accepting mainly ethnic Japanese. The same applies to India. Ethnically selective immigration has always been the norm. The IRG never asked the obvious question, should white Australians be offended by Asian countries such as Japan and India preferring immigrants of their own ethnicity? Neither did the IRG answer that question in the affirmative by protesting anti-white immigration policies.

Repeatedly, *Control or Colour Bar?* committed howlers, both of commission and omission, while steadfastly exuding confidence. This was as much a cynical ideological tract as it was a work of reason.

The crude Anglophobia of the pamphlet is indicated by another bald assertion: "It is a truism that humanity may wipe itself out unless the white race establishes a new relationship with the others." This was in 1960, when the nuclear standoff alluded to was between two predominantly white populations, the United States and the Soviet Union. The two other nuclear powers at that time were Britain and France. The first non-white power to acquire nuclear weapons was China, in 1964. Its ability to "wipe out" humanity has been slow to arrive, so clearly, the implication was that whites would destroy the world. As whites monopolised nuclear weapons in 1960, the pamphlet was implying that they were likely to attack non-white countries with nuclear weapons, something that had not happened since the Second World War when the United States used two fission bombs to end the war begun by racially supremacist Imperial Japan. The imputation was Anglophobic.

Cheap scare tactics, exaggerations and Anglophobic prejudice occurred throughout the pamphlet.

The IRG consisted largely of Anglo utopians who sought to strip Australia of the normal immigration protections. They also criticised America's protective immigration laws. The IRG was an early sign of cultural elites falling into confusion and effective hostility towards their own people. This led to the reckless policy of opening Australia's doors to global diversity.

Other IRG policies were unfriendly to Anglos. They behaved as though whites had no group interests, that it was wrong to seek to remain the majority, and that the disasters of ethno-religious diversity were not manifest around the world. More sinister was their decision to adopt a deceptive Fabian strategy to get around public opposition to Asian immigration. This ruthless strategy was evident in their escalating demands, and was made explicit by Arthur Stein, an American member. In a 1961 article titled "The Thin Edge of the Wedge", Stein explained that the IRG should begin by calling for small intakes of Asians, then call for more and more.[57] This showed zero respect for the democratic wishes of the majority Anglo population.

The Immigration Reform Group deserves criticism for denying or ignoring Anglo ethnic interests. Their scholarship was faulty. For example, they ignored the original rationale of restrictive immigration, formulated by philosopher John Stuart Mill and taken up and adapted to Australia by Sir Henry Parkes, long-time premier of New South Wales and the father of federation.[58]

The IRG members were academics in the soft social sciences and humanities – historians, sociologists, educationalists, and other academics – who should have known the intellectual basis of the White Australia Policy. As informed liberals they should have known that by the mid nineteenth century John Stuart Mill recognised ethnic interests and the conflict resulting from ethnic diversity. Sir Henry Parkes, the progressive premier of New South Wales, accepted

---

[57] Stein, Arthur. (1961). The thin edge of the wedge. *Prospect* (1): 23-24.

[58] Salter, F. K. (2020). Sir Henry Parkes's liberal-ethnic nationalism, *Sydney Trads: Weblog of the Sydney Traditionalist Forum*, https://sydneytrads.com/2020/12/18/sir-henry-parkess-liberal-ethnic-nationalism.

this argument and initiated the movement to federalise the colonies, an initiative that created the Australian Commonwealth. Yes, many wage-earners were motivated to support the policy not only for ethnic or cultural reasons but as a means to maintain decent wages and working conditions. But identity was also a powerful factor, as it has been for ethnic and nationalist movements around the world.[59]

By the 1950s, the soft social sciences in the U.S. had been captured by the cosmopolitan New Social Sciences. This has been documented by Eric Kaufmann in his book, *The Rise and Fall of Anglo America*.[60] It was not surprising therefore, that the IRG position on immigration became dominant in the universities. At no point did they subsequently acknowledge the criminal involvement in the liberal-isation of Australian immigration or the introduction of multiculturalism (as will be seen later on in Section C which covers Violence).

The popular historian Donald Horne (1921-2005, co-editor of intellectual magazine *Quadrant* from 1964 to 1966 was influenced by the Immigration Reform Group. Statements in his best known book, *The Lucky Country* (1964)[61] align with the IRG's reasoning and assumptions. Horne came to echo Hope's contempt for

---

[59] Salter, F. K. (2020). Sir Henry Parkes's liberal-ethnic nationalism, *Sydney Trads: Weblog of the Sydney Traditionalist Forum*, https://sydneytrads.com/2020/12/18/sir-henry-parkess-liberal-ethnic-nationalism/.

[60] Kaufmann, E. (2004). *The rise and fall of Anglo-America*. Cambridge, MA, Harvard University Press.

[61] Horne, D. (1966/1964). *The lucky country: Australia in the sixties*. Ringwood, Penguin.

Anglo Australia and his anxiety about national inferiority.

Horne's book is valuable for its impressions of the immigration reform movement of the late 1950s and early 1960s, which successfully agitated for the ending of the White Australia Policy. In particular he noted the IRG and its pamphlet *Control or Colour Bar?* He reported that the calls for reform (i.e., in favour of Asian immigration) were coming from the young university-educated generation in both the Liberal and Labor parties. He stated that a cause for this change of view largely originated in elite "opinion-forming quarters".[62] Indeed, public support for white immigration remained strong. Arthur Stein of the Immigration Reform Group complained in 1961 that only one newspaper, the *Melbourne Herald* (precursor to the *Herald-Sun*) editorialised against the White Australia Policy.[63]

In a footnote Horne stated that he had since changed his view in one respect: "I no longer agree that this policy does not damage us in Asian countries and I now think that a quota system, or some other restricted but public arrangement would be accepted as an improvement".[64] In subsequent pages he accepted other IRG views. He thought that Filipinos and rich Chinese from Hong Kong would pose no "risks of tension or destruction of ways of life" to Australia. He asserted that "an increased intake of Asian elites would certainly enrich Australian life". Most relevant to the

---

[62] Horne, *The lucky country*, p. 130.
[63] Stein, The thin edge of the wedge.
[64] Horne, *The lucky country*, p. 129.

present analysis, Horne expressed anti-English sentiment. He suggested that Asian elites would offset what he saw as the disproportionate English role in the universities.[65]

In a later book, *The Next Australia,* Horne continued his Anglophobia, criticising Australians' British identity and loyalty as a form of "master racism". Horne wanted to cut off Australia's national identity from its history.[66]

In *The Lucky Country*, Horne asserted that Australia could only be effective in Asian diplomacy if it reduced Asian "fears" by making visible changes to its immigration policy (i.e., by increasing the rate of Asian entry),[67] and asserted the defeatist version of the "yellow peril" fear subsequently adopted by Malcolm Fraser. This maintained that Australia has no choice but to allow Asian immigration; that it should, in effect, accept a subordinate status in relation to countries in the region, a status tolerated by no non-western country: "It is a task that will be undertaken either by Australians, or by someone else". This selectively pessimistic prognosis for Australian self-determination led Horne to a radical, one might say defeatist, conclusion that is now mainstream in the multicultural establishment. "My own view is that the future holds dramatic possibilities for Australia which

---

[65] Horne, *The lucky country*, pp. 131, 132.
[66] Horne (1971), *The next Australia*, pp. 25-26.
[67] Horne, *The lucky country,* p. 132.

may necessarily include racial change, that this is Australia's 'destiny'".[68]

We have already indicated that Horne's case is flawed. He displayed inconsistency. Consider his anti-English sentiment that Australia imported too many English university teachers. Horne thought this to be a problem because it contributed to the "serious alienation of Australian intellectuals from their own people." The solution? "We may need some Japanese, Indians, and Chinese to help break up the English influence". The unstated assumption is that students would be less alienated from Asian professors than from English ones, a strange logic given that most Australians in 1964 were of British ancestry. Why was Horne so prejudiced against the English?

---

[68] Horne, *The lucky country*, p. 132.

C-2. Are responsible or owe reparations for slavery or other harmful practices carried out by other Anglo or white people before they were born.

Uniquely, Anglo and white people are blamed today for slavery, despite the British being the first power to voluntarily end slavery, a process that began over 200 years ago. Slavery existed in the majority of ancient civilisations. From Ancient Egypt and Ancient Greece to the Ottoman Empire, slavery was normal. In the Islamic world slavery is written into its doctrine and has been widely practised for a millennium. Large numbers of Spanish people were enslaved when Spain was conquered by North African Muslims. White Europeans were frequently enslaved by African Barbary pirates up until the 19th century. This was the trigger for the French invasion of Morocco and the American invasion of Libya, both carried out to end the trade in white slaves.

To put the slave trade to North America in perspective, while that destination received 389,000 Africans between 1626 and 1865,[69] it has been estimated that more than one million Europeans, many from the British Isles, were sold into African slavery by Muslim slavers from 1530 to 1780.[70] Slavery still exists today in parts of Africa and Asia. This history of enslavement of Europeans is not taught or mentioned today and of

---

[69] Trans-Atlantic slave trade – estimates. https://slavevoyages.org/assessment/estimates, accessed 17.5.2021.

[70] Davis, R. C. (2003). *Christian slaves, Muslim masters: White slavery in the Mediterranean, the Barbary Coast, and Italy, 1500-1800*. London, Palgrave Macmillan.

course, no one suggests that people of African descent should pay for the actions of their ancestors. By contrast, Anglo and other white people today are held responsible for the slavery practised by members of their ethnic group long before anyone alive today was born. Financial reparations are being proposed. No other ethnic group is expected to make reparations for historical acts of aggression, conquest, or enslavement.

Another example of Anglophobia based on anti-colonialism is the movement for so-called "reconciliation" between indigenous and Anglo Australians. Advocates assert that due to their colonial past, Anglo Australians are solely responsible for indigenous grievances. They fail to acknowledge any grievance in the opposite direction. Political and media elites take for granted that to achieve reconciliation white Australians must apologise, pay reparations in the form of burdensome government social expenditure, change their behaviour, fly the separatist Aboriginal flag, allow their children to be shamed by the education system, and enshrine these and other impositions in the constitution.

C-3. Should have their children taught to believe that their own people, history, traditions and culture have transgressed the rights of non-European ethnic groups.

For decades now, schools and universities in Australia and elsewhere in the Anglosphere have been teaching white children to be ashamed of their history, culture and people. Australian schools fly the Aboriginal flag with the same visual prominence as the national flag. "Acknowledgement of Country" ceremonies are enforced at all public schools, a ritual that tells Anglo children that their country does not belong to them and that, by implication, their ancestors stole the land. Children are taught that whites and Anglos in particular have been responsible for suffering and dysfunction in many other communities.

The Rudd Labor government appointed Marxist historian Stuart Macintyre to write the national history curriculum. In 1999 Macintyre had written an openly Anglophobic text, *A Brief History of Australia*. In the final chapter he wished for the demographic displacement of Anglo Australians by Aborigines and Asians. Due to texts such as this, false histories of Aboriginal "genocide" and mistreatment are taught in schools, while counter-narratives such as Keith Windschuttle's 2002 book, *The Fabrication of Aboriginal History*, are ignored. Instead, students are routinely exposed to histories that criticise British colonisation and idealise pre-contact Aboriginal society. Examples include Bruce Pascoe's discredited

2014 book *Young Dark Emu*.[71] This theme is repeated in many historical and literary publications.

As recently as 2021, Kate Holden's book *The Winter Road*, offered explicitly anti-Anglo and anti-European criticisms of settler culture.[72] Holden, a regular contributor to the progressive press, mocked Australians' "morbid fixation" with hard working settler farmers. Even the wheat they grew "fitted wonderfully into the racist, nationalist, agrarian culture of White Australia on the eve of Federation". How could wheat evoke white racism? Because of its "biblical associations, its satiny fields, its satisfying ceremonies . . . , its European heritage and even its blondness". The book was favourably reviewed in the mainstream press. Historical reflection can be positive on the personal and societal levels, but it is not acceptable to present ideology and ethnic vilification as history. Attempts to put the history of western/European people in a positive light are opposed. For instance, efforts by the Ramsay Centre for Western Civilisation to promote the study of western civilisation were rejected by at least two leading Australian universities. At both the Australian National University and Sydney University staff were

---

[71] The children's edition was published in 2019. The original book was published in 2014 as: Bruce Pascoe (2014). *Dark emu: Black seeds: Agriculture or accident?*
For a forensic critique, see Sutton, P. and K. Walshe (2021). *Farmers or hunter-gatherers? The Dark Emu debate*. Melbourne, Melbourne University Press.

[72] Holden, K. (2021). *The winter road: A story of legacy, land and a killing at Croppa Creek*. Carlton, Victoria, Black Inc.

opposed to portraying western and Anglo identity in positive terms.[73]

Anti-Anglo hate is widespread in the Australian educational system. An example is Andrew Jakubowicz, a professor of sociology at the University of Technology Sydney, who uses tortuous Marxist theorising to frame Anglophobic ideas.[74] Typical of multicultural ideologues, Jakubowicz simultaneously calls for minorities to organise ethnically to advance their group interests while denying the legitimacy of white Australians doing the same. In particular, he advises Chinese-Australians to organise an ethnic lobby to oppose what he sees as a racist Anglo Australia.

Jakubowicz has a special problem with white Christian Australia. For example, he invidiously racialised the debate over section 18c of the Racial Discrimination Act by describing those opposed to this legislation as well-off white Christian men engaged in a "bigots' frenzy", "who are also the majority of those previously complained against under 18C".[75] He accused Australian journalists of suffering from too much

---

[73] Sixty staff at Sydney University objected to what they saw as a "masculinist, Anglocentric view of 'the West'" – Staff against the Ramsay Centre. An open letter to Michael Spence. 17.9.2018, accessed 14.5.2021.

[74] E.g. Jakubowicz, A. (2011). "Empires of the Sun: Towards a post-multicultural Australian politics." *Cosmopolitan Civil Societies Journal* 3(1): 65-85.

[75] Andrew Jakubowicz, A Bigots' Frenzy: how race, class and gender still matter in the Australian politics of Section 18C,*Pearls and Irritations* (blog) (11 November 2016) <johnmenadue.com> (accessed, 5 April 2017).

"whiteness" and advancing white-only narratives.[76] Nevertheless, Jakubowicz is routinely consulted by the mainstream media, including the Murdoch press, as an expert on ethnic affairs. He is embraced by the political establishment.

Many years ago, the professor was hired by the NSW government to create a website to provide resources with which schools should teach about multiculturalism. The site still exists, carrying Anglophobic lesson formats and literature. For example, the website criticises objections to Asianisation and excessive immigration, which it mocks with articles such as "Voices of the past in Anglo primal scream" by historian Peter Cochrane.[77] This contemptuous attitude towards white ethnic sentiment is typical of left multiculturalism upon which Jakubowicz has been a seminal influence.[78]

The Australian experience of Anglophobic school curricula is also apparent overseas. An example was provided by the British educationalist Calvin Robinson who reported observing anti-white racism in London

---

[76] Andrew Jakubowicz interviewed by Tracy Holmes, "When it comes to Whiteness in Australian media, we are still telling the same story", *ABC News Radio* (19 December 2016 at 14:14:52) <abc.net.au/newsradio> (accessed, 5 April 2017).

[77] Making multicultural Australia (2021). http://www.multiculturalaustralia.edu.au/library/media/Document/id/138.Voices-of-the-Past-in-Anglo-Primal-Scream, accessed 31 August 2021.

[78] Salter, F. K. (2018). "The inherent racism of SBS's multiculturalism, Part II. The academic experts." *SydneyTrads.com*: June, https://sydneytrads.com/2018/2006/2015/inherent-racism-of-multiculturalism-pt2011/.

schools in the 2010s, where whites were in the minority. Robinson concluded that British authorities work against parental values.[79] He saw the far-left indoctrination conducted across Britain as targeting white pupils and recommended that parents take their children out of school and educate them at home.

---

[79] Calvin Robinson: The left want to control ethnic minorities. Britain is not institutionally racist. New Culture Forum Channel, Youtube.com. https://www.youtube.com/watch?v=K1mI_2zTTNE&t=1126s, accessed 26.4.2021. From 12 minutes.
Also see https://www.calvinrobinson.org/, accessed 5.5.2021.

D. Are considered prone to racism according to the ideology of "Critical Race Theory", even when no direct evidence of racism exists.

Another accusation against Anglos is that white structural racism disadvantages non-whites socially and economically in Anglo or white societies. Whites are alleged to benefit from "white privilege". Evidence for this is thin, consisting of such outcomes as high indigenous imprisonment rates and lower incomes. The accusation is backed by "Critical Race Theory" (CRT), a Marxist ideology according to which "whiteness" should be seen as an exploitative class, not an ethnic group. This commonly repeated canard runs counter to scholarship on ethnicity described earlier, according to which ethnicities are descent groups, not income categories.

Furthermore, CRT claims that all non-white members of our society are oppressed because some, but not all, non-white ethnic groups have lower average wealth than the average white person. This is inconsistent with the evidence. For example, it ignores the fact that some non-whites and non-Anglos have a variety of cultural or other disadvantages which lower their economic outcomes compared to long-term citizens. Some indigenous people and recent arrivals from Third World countries have poor English and lower levels of education than most Australians, sometimes compounded by dysfunctional family relations. Critical Race Theory also ignores the fact that several non-Anglo ethnic groups have higher average incomes than whites. East Asians, Jews, Hindus and other groups have all fared well in western nations, often enjoying higher average incomes and status than whites. Typically, these groups do well at school, work hard and are supported by their families.

In Australia, large-scale surveys conducted under the auspices of the United Nations in 2018 and 2019 found that three quarters of Australians believe white people are discriminated against to some degree.[80] Significantly, the survey used Critical Race Theory to interpret its findings.[81] In the United States a 2017 poll found that 55 per cent of whites believed their ethnic group was being discriminated against. They also reported personally experiencing discrimination – 19 per cent when applying for jobs, 11 per cent when applying for college admission, and 13 per cent resulting in lower pay.[82]

In the case of the Australian survey, the United Nations' goal was to bring about "cultural, social, attitudinal and behavioural change".[83] In other words,

---

[80] Nicholas Faulkner, Kim Borg, Kun Zhao, and Liam Smith (2020). *The Inclusive Australia social inclusion index: 2020 report*, Monash University. https://inclusive-australia.s3.amazonaws.com/files/IA0013_Inclusive-Australia_Index2020_v6_single-pg-1.pdf, accessed 1.6.2021, Figures 6 and 7, pp. 17-18.

[81] *Inclusive Australia,* p. 13.

[82] Poll finds a majority of white Americans say discrimination against whites exists in America today, Press release, T. H. Chan School of Public Health, Harvard University, 7.11.2017. https://www.hsph.harvard.edu/news/press-releases/poll-white-americans-discrimination/, accessed 29.5.2021.

[83] *Inclusive Australia*, p. 6. The report carries the subheading: "Advancing the United Nations Sustainable Development Goals". Australia is a signatory. https://www.dfat.gov.au/aid/topics/development-issues/2030-

the Australian mainstream population, the majority of whom are Anglos, is judged by the UN to be so deplorable in ethnic attitudes that it needs re-education, even though they themselves face discrimination. Incredibly the Australian government agrees and collaborates. The survey report admitted that it had not asked about anti-white discrimination before 2018 and did so only because white perceptions of being discriminated against ethnically "may be driving [their] prejudice towards other minority groups".[84] The multicultural establishment shows little empathy for Anglo suffering.

No other ethnic group is treated in this way. Critical race theorists never describe Indian privilege or the wages of Japaneseness. Yet networking and favouritism are found in all ethnic groups. If Critical Race Theory was a genuine scholarly enterprise, it would compare ethnic networking and trust across a range of ethnicities, including those of the investigators. Whiteness studies has been Anglophobic from its inception in the 1960s, targeting and defaming whites and only whites.

The irrationality of whiteness studies comes from it being an ideology, not science or open-minded scholarship. The Black Lives Matter movement provides clear examples of irrationality, often tied to Critical Race Theory and the naked hatred of whites. In Australia, it is not true that Aboriginal deaths in custody are more frequent than the norm (discussed

---

agenda/Pages/sustainable-development-goals, accessed 1.6.2021.
[84] *Inclusive Australia,* p. 16.

below in Part B "Hostile Discrimination"). It is not true that whites are more prone to develop racist attitudes or, indeed, that western societies are burdened with such attitudes when compared to non-western societies, as discussed earlier regarding ethnocentrism and collectivism. It is obviously not true that defunding police will improve the lives of non-whites. Nowhere are BLM's claims more outrageous than in the universities and schools. The notion that marriage, or punctuality, or mathematics, are white constructs, is a fantasy.[85] The defamation and marginalisation of British Isles descended peoples has contributed to the growth of irrationality in the educational system and in public culture.

Critical Race Theory has helped normalise Anglophobic vilification, which has proliferated in the mainstream media and universities. A minor example indicates the ubiquity of Anglophobia and its corporate facilitators. Consider the ethnic slur "I just want to see less white mediocrity being rewarded". This comes from *The Weekend Australian* of 3 July 2021 in a review of the book *Hype* by Gabrielle Bluestone, published by the giant US corporation HarperCollins,

---

[85] Pasha-Robinson, L. (2017). Teaching maths perpetuates white privilege, says university professor. *The Independent*. London, 25 October, https://www.independent.co.uk/news/world/americas/teaching-maths-white-privilege-illinois-university-professor-rochelle-gutierrez-a8018521.html, accessed 16.10.2021.
Gray, A. (2019). The bias of 'professionalism' standards. *Stanford Social Innovation Review*, 4 June, https://ssir.org/articles/entry/the_bias_of_professionalism_standards, accessed 16.10.2021

a subsidiary of Rupert Murdoch's News Corporation.[86] A casual Anglophobic remark bears the imprimatur of Big Publishing and the Murdoch wing of Big Media. This was not an accidental slip. The review explains that Bluestone was quoting from a critic of the young blogger Caroline Calloway, who was characterised as a "very beautiful scumbag". The anti-whiteness quote comes next, implying that "very beautiful" mediocrities trade on nothing but their white privilege. However, the only picture of someone who trades on her beauty offered by the review is of model Bella Hadid, of Palestinian and Dutch descent. It should come as no surprise that models often come from outside the white world. The "white" in the remark was gratuitous.

The casualness of anti-Anglo and anti-white slurs is also evident in Britain, again aided by Critical Race Theory, as reported by Doug Stokes, a professor at Exeter University.[87] The British newspaper, *The Independent*, carried the subheading "When white men feel they are losing power, any level of nastiness is possible." The racist (and sexist) slur was prompted by reports that journalist Cathy Newman had been criticised on social media after she interviewed clinical

---

[86] Thornley, J. (2021). Don't believe the hype, just follow the money [review of Gabrielle Bluestone (2021). *Hype: How scammers, grifters and con artists are taking over the internet, and why we're following*, HarperCollins]. *The Weekend Australian*. 3 July: pp. 14-15,

[87] Stokes, D. (2021). Interview: Anti-white racism is rampant in universities, by Peter Whittle, 20 June, https://www.youtube.com/watch?v=Dlntg1qnyHM&t=65s.

psychologist Jordan Peterson in January 2018.[88] Peterson, a vocal opponent of racism and sexism, called this one of the most appalling headlines he had ever seen a credible news organisation produce.[89] (Critical Race Theory is further discussed in Section 5a below.)

Ironically, Critical Race Theory has enabled Structural Anglophobia, almost as if it was designed to do so. It has developed to such an extent that it has characteristics of an industry. There appears to be a market for anti-Anglo slurs powered by numerous individuals who perceive benefit in relaying and often amplifying the vilification. An anti-white infrastructure exists in the universities, media and government that uncritically repeats and sensationalises defamations. This infrastructure has been exploited by individuals who concoct stories of white racism. Once stated, structural Anglophobia does the rest.

A particularly egregious example from 2019 was provided by the black American actor Jussie Smollett, who told Chicago police that he had been attacked by two white men wearing MAGA hats (the slogan made famous by President Trump – "Make America Great

---

[88] Revesz, R. (2018). Misogynistic abuse against Cathy Newman is a symbol of the backlash against the MeToo movement. *Independent*. 21 January, accessed 16.8.2021.

[89] Peterson, Jordan (2019).
https://www.youtube.com/watch?v=qH1U9k0dwzI&t=1094s, accessed 21.7.2021. Posted 29 April 2019, from 18:12 minutes.

Peterson's interview by Cathy Newman can be viewed at:
https://www.youtube.com/watch?v=aMcjxSThD54, accessed 21.7.2021.

Again"). Smollett alleged that the men used anti-black and anti-gay taunts, poured an unknown substance over him, and hung a noose around his neck. The accusations were widely repeated by the mainstream media in the US and internationally.

Smollett was interviewed on American television by Robin Roberts who is herself of African American heritage and gave an entirely sympathetic interview in which she refrained from asking any tough questions. Roberts later explained that she was under pressure from different groups to put different slants on her report of Smollett's claims. "I'm a Black gay woman, he's a Black gay man, … He's saying that there's a hate crime, so if I'm too hard, then my LGBT community is going to say, 'You don't believe a brother,' if I'm too light on him, it's like, 'Oh, because you are in the community, you're giving him a pass.'"[90]

The alleged attack was presented as an example of rampant white racism. Democratic Party senators and Kamala Harris, then a candidate in the Democratic presidential primaries and a friend of Smollett's, described the alleged attack as an attempted lynching. Cory Booker, a Democratic senator for New Jersey, urged Congress to pass an anti-lynching bill with

---

[90] Kornick, L. (2021). ABC's 'Good Morning America' ignores Smollett trial despite giving sympathetic interview in 2019, *Fox News Network*, 30 November, https://www.foxnews.com/media/abc-good-morning-america-skips-jussie-smollett-trial, accessed 15.12.2021.

himself and Harris as co-sponsors.[91] All these individuals had personal or ethnic interests in supporting Smollett's racial libel against white Trump supporters.

In December 2021 Smollett was found guilty by a US court of lying to police. The prosecution's star witnesses were the two black accomplices Smollett had hired to stage the attack.[92] The motive appears to have been at least partly commercial. Police alleged that Smollett hoped that he would receive a higher salary if it were believed that he was the victim of white racism and President Trump. The accomplices concurred with this allegation by stating that Smollett staged the attack because a threatening letter he received a week earlier (which was sent by himself) failed to produce as much attention as he had hoped.[93]

For decades the Anglophobia industry has been ready to condemn white people for alleged racist crimes. The Smollett case is the most recent in a series of media

[91] Anapol, Avery (2019). Kamala Harris: Violent attack on 'Empire' star is 'attempted modern day lynching', The Hill, 29 January 2019. https://thehill.com/homenews/senate/427538-kamala-harris-violent-attack-on-empire-star-is-attempted-modern-day-lynching, accessed 14.12.2021.

[92] Gbogbo, Mawunyo (2021). Empire actor Jussie Smollett found guilty of orchestrating fake attack on himself, *ABC News,* 10 December, https://www.abc.net.au/news/2021-12-10/jussie-smollett-verdict-guilty/100685594.

[93] Francescani, Chris, Stephanie Wash, and Eva Pilgrim (2019). Judge sets $100,000 bond for Jussie Smollett, orders 'Empire' actor's passport surrendered, ABC News, 22 February. https://abcnews.go.com/US/jussie-smollett-custody-chicago-police-allegedly-lying-attack/story?id=61208295. accessed 14.12.2021.

sensations fuelled by leftist politicians and minority activists such as Reverends Jesse Jackson and Al Sharpton, and Barack Obama. Examples include the Tawana Brawley rape allegations of 1987, the Duke Lacrosse allegations of 2006, and the Trayvon Martin murder trial of 2012. In all cases, white America was vilified by establishment media and politicians.

D-1. Are considered guilty of holding "white supremacist" beliefs for simply expressing or advocating on behalf of white or Anglo identity.

Racial supremacy is the belief that a particular people are better than all others and should rule over or dominate other races. This chauvinistic ideology has motivated conquest down the ages by aggressors of many ethnicities and races. Whites, of course, are not exempt. Supremacist notions were in evidence during the period of European colonialism. Since the mid twentieth century, however, radical ideologues began using the term "supremacist" to describe defensive as well as offensive attitudes, and applied it exclusively to whites. Today, anyone indicating even the mildest defence or advocacy of white or Anglo people risks being accused of a laundry list of epithets. No other group is subject to such extreme labelling for simply advocating the rights of their group or defending their group against attack. For instance, when Senator Pauline Hanson put up the motion that "It's alright to be white" in the Australian Senate, the Australian Greens leader Richard Di Natale said the "it's OK to be white" slogan had a long history in the white supremacist movement.[94] This is typical of the anti-white racism displayed by multicultural advocates.

As sociologist Eric Kaufmann points out in his book, *Whiteshift*, since the 1960s, multiculturalist

---

[94] "Pauline Hanson's 'It's OK to be white' motion narrowly defeated in Senate", *The Guardian*, 16.10.2018. https://www.theguardian.com/australia-news/video/2018/oct/16/pauline-hansons-its-ok-to-be-white-motion-narrowly-defeated-in-senate-video, accessed 4.6.2021.

governments and social movements have routinely suppressed white identity. They have treated Anglos as a common enemy against which to mobilise, instead of including them as a legitimate part of the multicultural mix who deserve the right to cherish and defend their identity. Though it is normal for other ethnic groups to identify with their heritage, too often Anglos have been browbeaten into not doing the same.[95]

Even depictions of homogeneous Anglo society are treated as suspicious and have been driven out of popular culture. An example is the British television series *Midsomer Murders* based on the series of novels *Chief Inspector Barnaby* written by Caroline Graham. The setting is Midsomer, a fictional modern English county. First broadcast in 1997, the program became popular around the world, especially in Anglophone countries. Arguably its popularity was largely due to the Englishness of the setting and characters. This interpretation was stated by Brian True-May, one of the two founding producers. In a 2011 interview, True-May explained that the program did not have non-white characters because he had created Midsomer to be a "bastion of Englishness". The formula had succeeded in attracting a large audience. He also implied that Englishness was its own ethnic category that was distinct from other ethnic identities.

True-May was summarily suspended as producer and only reinstated after offering an apology. Soon afterwards he stepped down. Asian characters then began to appear in the program. The removal of True-

---

[95] Kaufmann, E. (2018). *Whiteshift: Populism, immigration, and the future of white majorities*, Penguin.

May was driven by ITV, Britain's oldest commercial television network and the purchaser of the *Midsomer Murders* series. ITV declared that it was "shocked and appalled".[96] At no point did True-May defame non-Anglos. He was catering to market demand for portrayals of English society, a laudable undertaking if multicultural ideology is to be believed and freedom of association retained. True-May's openness hinted at the arbitrariness of his punishment. "We are a cosmopolitan society in this country, but if you watch Midsomer you wouldn't think so." . . . "I've never been picked up on that, but quite honestly I wouldn't want to change it."

No other ethnic group is forbidden from making movies expressly for and by its members. One popular film review website happily lists 115 of the best black movies of all time.[97] "We defined Black films as those that centred on African American stories and African American characters, or – as in the case of *Black Panther* – were made by Black filmmakers and were embraced by African American audiences." The review praised *Moonlight*, a film with an all-black cast that won best picture at the 2017 Academy Awards. Why not? The idea that Indian or Chinese or African film companies would be condemned for making movies without minority ethnic actors is ridiculous. Alone in the world, Anglos in particular, and whites more generally, have for decades been under pressure

---

[96] "Midsomer producer to step down' after current series", *BBC News*, 23.3.2011. https://www.bbc.com/news/entertainment-arts-12830475, accessed 28.5.2021.

[97] "The 115 best black movies of the 21st century". Celebrating black history. e, accessed 31.5.2021.

to not make films exclusively for, or about, their own ethnic groups.

More damaging is the falsification of British and white social history in recent movies. Casting black people as prominent members of Queen Elizabeth I's and Mary Queen of Scots' courts (e.g. *Mary Queen of Scots*, 2018), having Winston Churchill converse with a black Londoner in the Underground in 1940 (*Darkest Hour*, 2017), or showing non-whites as normal in Medieval Europe (*Anne Boleyn*, 2021; *Cinderella*, 2021; *A Knight's Tale*, 2001; *Robin Hood: Men in Tights*, 1993; *Horrible Histories*[98]), are social lies.[99] And they are not small lies, even in the case of comedies. Since the early twentieth century, film has been the most popular and persuasive form of mass entertainment. Film influences public understanding of mores and national identity. It is therefore a small but palpable act of cultural genocide, whether deliberate or not, to cast actors whose ethnicity misrepresents ancestral society. It steals people's history. As George

---

[98] E.g. 'Been here from the start' song, Horrible Histories. *Black British History | CBBC,* 12 Oct. 2021. https://www.youtube.com/watch?v=6M-qsVS8zeU, accessed 8.11.2021.

[99] Williams, T. (2018). 'Mary Queen of Scots' fact check: Was Queen Elizabeth's ambassador actually black?, *The Wrap*, 25 December, https://www.thewrap.com/mary-queen-of-scots-fact-check-was-queen-elizabeth-ambassador-actually-black/, accessed 20.10.2021.

Gleiberman, Owen. (2017). The London Underground scene of "Darkest Hour': So false, so winning, so slam-dunk Oscar, *Variety*, 25 November, https://variety.com/2017/film/columns/darkest-hour-underground-scene-gary-oldman-1202622763/, accessed 20.10.2021.

Orwell explained in his dystopian novel, *1984*, "Who controls the past controls the future: who controls the present controls the past."

Western audiences are tolerant of subtle racial differences in roles. They also tolerate non-whites being cast to play a role originally cast as white but which is not historically associated with whiteness. An example is *The Equalizer* (2014), which was originally written for a white lead but was played by African-American Denzel Washington to popular acclaim. Non-whites are free to develop their own cinema, and they do so, producing overtly non-white movies, as noted above.

The falsification of Anglo history is a form of Anglophobia. Anglos and other European-descended peoples will not be able to claim and hold their identities without making historically correct movies. That will not be possible until the Anglophobic bias of film producers and distributors is abolished.

D-2. Are uniquely culpable for racism due to their power over non-whites always and everywhere.

A common Anglophobic nostrum is that only whites can be racist because racism entails power. It is contended that blacks and other non-whites cannot be racist because they lack power. This proposition has some obvious limits. For example, Anglos and whites have minimal presence in nations like China, India, and most of Africa. Even in western nations, the power of the white majority has declined markedly. Prior to the 1970s, Australia and America had immigration policies that favoured whites, keeping them an overwhelming majority of the population. These policies were removed by powerful progressive elites without support from the majority who have never been allowed to vote on them. The result has been a decline in Anglos' share of the population and therefore a decline in their voting and political power.

For decades, restricting the power of non-Anglos in Anglosphere nations has been illegal and increasingly unacceptable culturally. Non whites have had no legal impediments and few other limitations placed on their pursuit of power. Minorities and their champions have been able to rise politically both locally and federally. In neighbourhoods where minorities form majorities, local government positions are often dominated by non-Anglos thanks to tribal voting patterns.

In the United States, Barack Obama, an African American, was able to serve two terms as US president, thanks in part to these tribal minority voting patterns. Fully 95 percent of African Americans voted for him in a record turnout as did approximately two thirds of

Hispanics and Asians. By contrast, in a country where white identity had been suppressed for generations by the media and educational establishments, the white vote was roughly split, with only moderately more voting for McCain, the white Republican candidate, than for Obama.[100] The white vote continues to be split, though the lean towards the Republican Party has risen in recent elections.

With the white vote only moderately leaning towards the Republicans, political parties were able to take those voters for granted, while at the same time fielding minority candidates and whites who cater to minority interests in the hope of attracting their votes. This voting power has contributed to the pro-minority legislation and the promotion of non-white immigration aimed at increasing the Democratic vote.[101]

Non-Anglos are filling positions of power in other areas such as business and the bureaucracy, sometimes aided by affirmative action that operates to reduce white advancement. In America, numerous Democrat cities with large minority populations often have political positions such as mayors, police chiefs and district attorneys dominated by minorities. Many giant corporations and tech companies are owned or run by

---

[100] Lopez, M. H. and P. Taylor (2009). Dissecting the 2008 electorate: Most diverse in U.S. history. Washington D.C., Pew Research Center, https://www.pewresearch.org/wp-content/uploads/sites/5/reports/108.pdf, accessed 17.2.2022.

[101] Bowler, S. and G. M. Segura (2010). *The future is ours: Minority politics, political behavior, and the multiracial era of American politics*. Los Angeles, Sage.

minorities or migrants, as one would expect in an open economy.

The idea that non-whites can never wield power in traditionally white nations is therefore without merit. Almost anyone can wield local power. An example of local power is anyone showing hostility towards vulnerable individuals, whether by shouting abuse, assaulting them, or refusing to hire or promote them. Such acts are racist when they are motivated in part or in full by ethnic animus, regardless of whether or not the discriminator's group is overall more numerous, wealthy, powerful, or educated.

One example of a powerful individual expressing racist sentiments towards whites was provided recently by Professor Brittney Cooper, an African American tenured professor at New Jersey's Rutgers University. Cooper teaches classes on women's, gender and African studies.

In an online interview Cooper stated that,

> "I think that white people are committed to being villains... they are *so* corrupt, you know, their thinking is so morally and spiritually bankrupt about power...The thing I want to say to you is we gotta take these motherf****s out, but I know, but like, we can't say that.... White folks are not infinite ... it has an end, and so part of what we are trying to do is to imagine, what are the steps that

we must take to get to the other side of this very inconvenient, you know, epochal interruption."[102]

In American parlance, to "take out" people means to kill them. At its worst, the language used in this quote could be construed to be genocidal. In another public statement, while defending Critical Race Theory, Cooper denied she was advocating violence, but expressed approval of the low white birth rate.[103] Even taken at its most positive, this is an example of extreme racial hatred.

The claim that outbursts such as Cooper's are not racist because they come from individuals who lack power on account of their African heritage, is implausible to say the least. Professors possess the prestige of their rank and title and have real power over their students. They stand to influence young people who will go on to become professionals and occupy leadership positions. Power is also indicated by the fact that the Professor was able to make eliminationist racist comments without facing any disciplinary consequences. Leftist media outlets such as the

---

[102] Alex Hammer and Shannon Thaler (2021). Rutgers University fails to condemn tenured professor who said 'we got to take these motherf*****s out' about white people, *Daily Mail*, 30 October, https://www.dailymail.co.uk/news/article-10145969/Public-furious-Rutgers-professor-Brittney-Coopers-history-anti-white-comments.html?ito=native_share_article-masthead

[103] Poff, Jeremiah (2021). Rutgers professor says white people deserve low birth rates, *Washington Examiner*, 28 October, https://news.yahoo.com/rutgers-professor-says-white-people-153000065.html, accessed 17.2.2022.

Huffington Post supported her remarks.[104] The Rutgers branch of the American Association of University Professors and the American Federation of Teachers as well as the AFL-CIO union federation expressed "solidarity" with Cooper's right to free speech, denied that she advocated violence, praised her research into white supremacism, and accused her critics of "trying to silence people of color".[105] The majority of mainstream media outlets failed to report Cooper's remarks, apart from *Fox News* and the *Daily Mail*.

Were a white professor to make disparaging comments about black people, even with ambiguous phrases, he would be lucky to keep his job. There are many examples of white academics, teachers and administrators in the U.S. being criticised for using a word "niggardly" on the false assumption that it is an ethnic slur. Greg Patton, Professor of Business Communication, was suspended after a student complained that his pronunciation of the Chinese word for "that" sounded like "nigger".[106] Patton did not have

---

[104] Ross, Lawrence (2021). Brittney Cooper's truth-telling is too much for the cowardly right-wing mob, *The Huffington Post*, 8 November. https://www.huffpost.com/entry/brittney-cooper-racist-right-wing-mob_n_61887ea0e4b055e47d7c0af0, accessed 17.2.2022.

[105] Rutgers AAUP-AFT statement in solidarity with Brittney Cooper, 5 November 2021, https://rutgersaaup.org/rutgers-aaup-aft-statement-in-solidarity-with-brittney-cooper/, accessed 17.2.2022.

[106] Controversy over USC professor's use of Chinese word that sounds like racial slur in English, *Los Angeles Times*, 5 September 2020. https://www.latimes.com/california/story/2020-09-05/usc-business-professor-controversy-chinese-word-english-slur, accessed 18.2.2022.

enough power to save himself from an absurd accusation.

Patton's case contrasts with an absence of disciplinary action against Cooper for overtly racist statements. The power of her position is further indicated by the institutional support she received. Cooper was a privileged beneficiary of America's multicultural political establishment, receiving what Critical Race Theory, if it were unbiased scholarship, would label the "wages of blackness".

D-3. Must be racist because they are on average wealthier, healthier, or better educated than some other racial or ethnic groups.

Critical Race Theory helps establish structural Anglophobia. It is aided in doing so by a much older aspect of leftist ideology. That is the insistence that cultural and racial differences do not contribute to inequality, whether social or economic. The ideology originates from the utopian wish for universal equality. Unfortunately, it has implications. Proponents of this line of thinking argue that whites do not have any cultural or genetic advantages over non-whites. Any differences in wealth, health, or education are therefore assumed to be due to "disadvantage", which includes racism enabled by the assumed ubiquitous power of whites. The same idea is often expressed in terms of "white supremacy". It is claimed that there can be no cultural or racial explanations for class differences between whites and non-whites, because to make that suggestion implies that one type of people is superior and the other inferior, a notion that is immoral and therefore not true.

These claims commit factual and logical errors. To summarise, ethnic differences not only exist; they are the norm. Differences are typically minor; but can be substantial. Group differences in talent, wealth, and health are caused partly by cultural and genetic differences, as well as by historical and geographical luck. Anglos and other whites rate higher than some populations, and lower than others. Finally, the argument commits a logical error, the moralistic fallacy. This is the attempt to derive factual claims from moral precepts. Unfortunately, just because a proposition is unpleasant, does not mean it is factually incorrect.

Let us briefly review the evidence for white merit – and demerit.

Culture

The different peoples that came into contact during the colonial period around what would become the Anglosphere brought with them centuries of accumulated culture. The participants were often unequal, because their cultures were different. The contrast was stark with regard to material culture. The British had muskets and cannon, horse-drawn wagons, and printing. In the case of Australian settlement, they were already in the process of industrialising.

Historian Geoffrey Blainey explains that when the British First Fleet sailed into Sydney Harbour in January 1788, it inaugurated contact between very different cultures. "The people who had just invented the steam engine were face-to-face with people who, though rich in many branches of knowledge, could not boil water." [107]

Two centuries later, differences in material culture have receded, but inequality remains. In every settler society the indigenous people are substantially poorer than the descendants of the European settlers. The

---

[107] Blainey, G. (2018). Australia Day doubters misread our past. *The Australian.* Sydney, 25 January, https://www.theaustralian.com.au/commentary/opinion/australia-day-doubters-misreadour-past/news-story/a4ffd4e49074343a7c24fb1eb120e127, accessed 29.11.2021.

cause is unlikely to be white racism because several immigrant groups have overtaken Anglos in average earnings and other measures of prestige. Could non-material aspects of culture advantage Anglos and other European-descended peoples? And could this help explain the extraordinary technological edge held by Anglos over native peoples in earlier centuries? The question of cultural advantage has spurred research among historians and social scientists, much of it directed at other ethnic, religious, and national inequalities.

The German sociologist, Max Weber, in his famous 1905 book *The Protestant Ethic and the Spirit of Capitalism*, tried to explain the rise of capitalism in Northern Europe as being due to religious differences between Protestants and Catholic. Weber thought that Protestantism was better attuned to capitalism. Right or wrong, the book opened a debate that continues today. Weber introduced the concept of work ethic and thus cultural influences on economic behaviour. Another German analyst, Werner Sombart, in his 1911 book *The Jews and Modern Capitalism,* thought Judaism was the front-runner.

Weber argued that capitalism was the application of legal-rational thinking to business. He saw this as a modern phenomenon manifested in Protestant Northern Europe. His thesis fitted the Enlightenment dogma that scientific and industrial progress had to overcome Catholic resistance. The more radical version of Weber's thesis is that agnostic and atheist beliefs facilitate science and business.

An alternative theory, as proposed by historian Rodney Stark for example, is that Christianity was the midwife of European modernisation. While there are well known examples of the Catholic Church resisting some scientific ideas, the broader story is one of institutional nurture and encouragement. Across the continent the Church founded the first universities. For centuries scientists believed that by logic and observation they were revealing the marvel of God's creation. Christianity thus emphasised truth as a goal in itself. It also buttressed individual responsibility. The effect was social as well as creative. Stark argues that together, these effects of Christianity helped the West pull ahead of the rest of the world by the end of the Middle Ages.[108] Stark's account also points to the importance of individualism, another culturally-enhanced difference between expanding Europeans and the peoples they encountered around the world.

Canadian sociologist Ricardo Duchesne presents another approach to understanding the source of the West's outward urge, wealth, industry, scientific discovery, and military power. In his 2011 book *The Uniqueness of Western Civilization*, Duchesne argues that the West has achieved a number of firsts, such as the enforcement of elite monogamy, the era of worldwide exploration, the philosophical and Scientific Revolutions, the Renaissance, the development of constitutional government and plural institutions, the establishment of globe-spanning

---

[108] Stark, R. (2006). *The victory of reason: How Christianity led to freedom, capitalism, and Western success*. New York, Random House.

empires and trading systems, the repudiation of slavery, the Industrial Revolution, and the elevation of women's rights. He points out that those who would censor knowledge of cultural group differences are typically critical of western interests in general and Anglo interests in particular. Their thrust is to discourage pride in western achievement by denying merit as an explanation for western advance. They attribute the success of European populations to theft through colonialism or taking ideas from other civilisations such as China.[109] They seek to belittle unique achievements.

Whatever the origins of the West's cultural achievements – and many of those cited above obviously had their beginnings in Europe – they appear to have conferred advantages on peoples belonging to the Anglo and western traditions.

Genes

Different evolutionary histories have produced genetic diversity among human populations. The diversity is most apparent when comparing continental-scale populations (races). Consequently, instead of discussing Anglos, this section reviews data gathered on their encompassing population, the indigenous peoples of Europe and their descendants.

Race coincides with dozens of physiological charac-teristics, produced during development accor-ding to genetic blueprints. Some of these characteristics are so obvious that computers can accurately identify an

---

[109] Duchesne, Ricardo (2011). *The uniqueness of Western civilization*, Leiden/Boston, Brill.

individual's race from photographs.[110] That might not seem very special. After all, humans can also recognise racial identity from such clues as skin colour, hair form, and facial features. However, computers can do something humans cannot. They can detect race by inspecting mammograms and x-rays of hands and chests.[111]

It follows that race is not "a social construct" as our best and brightest are taught in school and university. Races are biological populations. They are similar, of course, due to them belonging to the same species but also different because of separation through evolutionary time and being naturally selected by different environments. As a result of their evolutionary history, the genetic similarity of random members of the same race is surprisingly high, typically equivalent to first cousins or closer, depending on the races being compared.[112]

The case of unequal health outcomes between Australian Aborigines and their Anglo counterparts appears to be caused in part by genetic differences, a factor unrelated to racism. Until 1788 all Australian Aborigines lived as hunter-gatherers. Northern Europeans exited that lifestyle about 5,000 years ago,

---

[110] https://www.wsj.com/articles/the-quiet-growth-of-race-detection-software-sparks-concerns-over-bias-11597378154, accessed 24.11.2021.

[111] Banerjee, I. and et al. (2021). Reading race: AI recognises patient's racial identity in medical images, *arXiv.org*, 21 July, https://arxiv.org/abs/2107.10356, accessed 24.11.2021.

[112] Salter, F. K. (2007/2003). *On genetic interests: Family, ethnicity, and humanity in an age of mass migration*. New Brunswick, N.J., Transaction Publishers.

when they adopted Near Eastern agriculture. Due to these different histories, hunter gatherers have less ability to digest refined carbohydrates than populations whose ancestors depended on agriculture for thousands of years. Now that most Aborigines consume a western diet, they typically suffer a range of adverse health outcomes such as higher rates of diabetes and vulnerability to alcohol, which exacerbates domestic violence. Sedentary lifestyle and obesity also contribute to diabetes. Dr Alan Barclay of the Australian Diabetes Council has attributed the early onset of diabetes in Aborigines to an evolutionary history that did not include agriculture.[113] John Boulton, a medical researcher specialising in Aboriginal paediatrics, believes that we need to draw on evolutionary biology to better understand and treat the health disaster that has afflicted outback Aboriginal communities for generations.[114] This approach has had some success in Canada, where researchers have identified a gene predisposing the indigenous population of Manitoba to diabetes.[115]

A similar situation exists regarding cow milk, which most of the world's populations find difficult to digest.

---

[113] Dr. Alan Barclay was interviewed by Alan Jones, Radio 2GB, 9 July 2012.

[114] Nicolas Rothwell, "Genes key to health gone awry", *Weekend Australian*, 1-2 June 2013, Inquirer, p. 15.

[115] Millar, K. and H. J. Dean (2012). "Developmental origins of Type 2 diabetes in Aboriginal youth in Canada: It is more than diet and exercise." *Journal of Nutrition and Metabolism* 2012, https://www.hindawi.com/journals/jnme/2012/127452/, accessed 25.11.2021.

Lactose is the sugary component of milk. Digesting it requires an enzyme, lactase, which is produced by all human babies. The relevant gene is switched off before the individual reaches adulthood, except in those parts of the world where cow herding has been common. This includes large parts of Europe, especially north of the Alps. In that population, the lactase gene is not switched off and adults can consume milk. This is considered a classic example of gene-culture evolution, where culture (herding and milk consumption) selects for genes (coding for lactase), which then facilitate an intensification of the culture.[116] Adult Aborigines, like Chinese and Africans, are often allergic to milk. A 1983 study found that 80 percent of full-blood Aborigines, but only 20 percent of non-Aboriginal controls, showed malabsorption of cow milk. The percentages showing abdominal pain or diarrhoea were 64 and 20, respectively.[117] Today, thankfully, milk can be avoided, and lactose-free milk is commercially available.

Despite high levels of government expenditure on Australian Aboriginal welfare, including health services, their evolutionary history combined with radically changed environment often causes poor health outcomes.

---

[116] Cavalli-Sforza, L. L. (1986). Cultural evolution and genetics. *Human genetics: Proceedings of the 7th International Congress Berlin 1986*. F. Vogel and K. Sperling. Berlin, Springer: 24-33.

[117] Brand, J. C., M. S. Gracey, R. M. Spargo and S. P. Dutton (1983). Lactose malabsorption in Australian Aborigines. *American Journal of Clinical Nutrition* 37(3): 449-452.

Superior health is one advantage Anglos and other Australians descended from farmers or cow herders frequently have over many people of indigenous heritage. Genes predispose some populations, without conscious effort, to be better (*not* perfectly!) adapted to a diet that includes carbohydrates, alcohol, and cow milk. Such a population will tend to enjoy a healthier, longer, and more productive life. It is wrong to view the resulting inequality as evidence of "white supremacy". By the 1990s sufficient data had accumulated to show that many racial differences, including physiology and behaviour, fall into a broad pattern in which Europeans, on average, score between East Asians and sub-Saharan Africans. This was the finding of the late Philippe Rushton, a Canadian professor of psychology. If his results are correct, there is no scientific basis for an absolutist white supremacism.[118] Rushton's findings also apply to intelligence, as measured by IQ tests.

No topic is more controversial than race and IQ. A taboo is enforced against any attempt to use IQ differences to explain racial differences in economic or educational outcomes. Such attempts are understandable because, firstly, there are persistent race differences in IQ and, secondly, IQ is the single largest correlate of educational success. This point is well documented in *The Bell Curve: Intelligence and Class Structure in American Life*, a book authored by Richard Herrnstein and Charles Murray in 1994. Herrnstein died around the time the book was

---

[118] Rushton, J. P. (1995). *Race, evolution, and behavior*. New Brunswick, NJ, Transaction Publishers.

published, leaving Murray to answer critics alone. *The Bell Curve* caused a raging controversy, because it reported the well-known 15-point average IQ difference between whites and blacks in the United States. Furthermore, it pointed out that whites and blacks of equal IQ have similar incomes. This suggests that the disparity between the races is not due to white racism but to merit. If this had become accepted by the public, the identity politics industry would have lost its most bankable victim.

Accusations of white supremacism were levelled at Murray, though *The Bell Curve* implied that Anglos do not have the highest IQ or the greatest incomes. In fact, East Asians and Jews have average IQs above those of whites in the US, with correspondingly higher incomes. Like Rushton, Murray's book placed whites on a spectrum, but not supreme. Why then should his theory be branded as "white supremacist"?

This pattern repeats itself outside the US The most comprehensive source of IQ scores around the world is *Race Differences in Intelligence: An evolutionary Analysis*, written by British psychologist Richard Lynn in 2005. Lynn was the first to report the elevated IQs of East Asians.[119] He also found that the correlation between IQ and income applied globally, in *IQ and the Wealth of Nations* (2002). The book, co-authored with Finnish sociologist Tatu Vanhanen, reported that per capita GDP was correlated substantially with the average IQ of the population.

---

[119] Lynn, R. (1977). The intelligence of the Japanese. *Bulletin of the British Psychological Society* 30: 69-72.

Some of the foregoing scientific issues are not fully resolved, though theories of cultural and genetic influence have gained strength as research accumulates. Despite the support of many experts, hypotheses of cultural and genetic influences on ethnic differences in health, wealth and educational attainment have been written off. Once again, the debate had been won not by facts or logic but by censorship and intimidation. The media's misreporting of the controversy over *The Bell Curve* was so pronounced that 52 academics specialising in IQ research published a letter in the *Wall Street Journal* in 1994. The letter was written by Linda Gottfredson, professor of educational psychology.[120] The letter pointed out that most of *The Bell Curve*'s assumptions were mainstream, such as the black-white IQ difference, the accuracy of IQ tests, and their correlation with educational, occupational, economic, and social outcomes.

The savage reception of *The Bell Curve* was a repeat of that accorded to educational psychologist Arthur Jensen in 1969 when he suggested that the black-white IQ difference was partly genetic. An analysis of that controversy by Mark Snyderman and Stanley Rothman in 1984 found that the media had misrepresented scientific opinion.[121] Most leading psychologists agreed with the core tenets of Jensen's theory of the

---

[120] Gottfredson, L. S. (1997). "Mainstream science on intelligence: An editorial with 52 signatories, history, and bibliography." *Intelligence* 24(1): 13-23.

[121] Snyderman, M. and S. Rothman (1988). *The IQ controversy: The media and public policy*. New York, Transaction Books.

black-white IQ difference, a view repeated by Herrnstein and Murray (1994). Most believed that IQ measures scholastic ability, that it is substantially heritable, and that IQ differences contribute to socioeconomic differences including those between blacks and whites.

Snyderman and Rothman found only one expert on race and IQ, Leon Kamin, of the Boasian school of anthropology, who rejected genetic effects altogether as a cause of racial IQ differences. They identified a strong bias in the media and among intellectuals against the hereditarian view despite it being in the scientific mainstream. They concluded that biased members of the cultural elite were the drivers of this distortion – academics, civil rights activists and social service professionals who advocated liberal progressive ideas. They found that radicals such as Kamin and Stephen Jay Gould were regularly and falsely portrayed in the media as representing the mainstream scientific view. They also found evidence of anti-white racism. For example, the aforementioned activists maintained that hereditarian theory was the product of a pronounced bias on the part of middle-class whites.[122]

A similar pattern of irrationality occurred in Australia. Senior Murdoch journalist Greg Sheridan, whose Anglophobia is described below (Section 5a), entered the debate over *The Bell Curve* on the far-left side. In a tirade that demonstrated incomprehension, he accused Murray of being "morally offensive" and "a

---

[122] Snyderman and Rothman, pp. 18, 182.

plausible statistical manipulator", likened his work to "Nazi pseudo-science", and called his thesis "perverse". He summarised *The Bell Curve* as "a mumbo-jumbo amalgam of pseudo-science and highly dodgy statistics with, so far as I can see, zero intellectual credibility".[123] Sheridan declared that Murray's methods, "such as they are", were inapplicable in Australia because "we don't do IQ tests" and furthermore, "we do not really have identifiable, self-sustaining racial groups". This kind of vituperation, combined with censorship, has helped shut down much rational examination of race and ethnicity in Australia since the 1960s.

Sadly, intimidation has played an important role in suppressing research on racial differences. Scholars are unable to mention or investigate ethnic differences without risking their reputations and livelihoods. There are many examples, but for the sake of brevity we shall examine just two.

Jason Richwine, who completed his doctorate at Harvard University, was forced to resign from his position in the Heritage Foundation in 2013 for using research on race differences in IQ to understand how immigrants integrate into American society.[124]

In 2019 a young Cambridge academic, Noah Carl, was fired for conducting research into race and intelligence.

---

[123] Sheridan, G. (1994). Genetic inferiority just mumbo-jumbo. *The Australian*. Sydney, 2 November.

[124] Richwine, Jason (2013, 9 August). Why can't we talk about IQ? *Politico.com*, 9 August, https://www.politico.com/story/2013/08/opinion-jason-richwine-095353, accessed 24.11.2021.

Carl was criticised in an open letter signed by hundreds of Cambridge academics. He was defended by few. The reasons stated for the sacking included Carl's attending a scientific meeting on race and intelligence and thereby associating with individuals who had conducted research unacceptable to the Cambridge mainstream.[125] This act of political intolerance and intellectual thuggery override ancient scholarly standards and rejected anything that might show the indigenous population of England collectively in a good light. Like Australia's universities, Cambridge has been colonised by intolerant Anglophobic ideologues.

To prevent a man from claiming merit as explanation for his success is to imply that he has been lucky or has cheated. Similarly, it is implicitly Anglophobic to impose a blanket denial that Anglos have done well partly due to merit.

In society as a whole, it does appear that Anglos and other peoples of European descent have achieved their place in society largely through talent and work. Some other ethnic groups outperform whites in IQ tests, education, and earnings, and do so within western countries. Taking these facts together, there is no evidence that white supremacism is a significant force in contemporary white societies. If it were so, how could Anglophobic multiculturalism survive?

---

[125] Adams, R. (2019). Cambridge college sacks researcher over links with far right. *The Guardian*. London, 2 May. https://www.theguardian.com/education/2019/may/01/cambridge-university-college-dismisses-researcher-far-right-links-noah-carl, accessed 25.11.2021.

The persecution of those who attempt to research racial differences leaves radicals free to attribute the poor outcomes experienced by some ethnic groups to Anglo racism and discrimination. Furthermore, the radicals emphasise only one kind of "supremacism". They decry white ethnocentrism while ignoring the ethnocentrism of all other peoples. This singling out of whites – the starting position of Critical Race Theory (see Section 4, 5a) – is itself a form of racism.

What is white supremacy, anyway? Supremacism is ill defined. It can mean *belief* in superiority as a matter of fact, whether racial, cultural. or political. Or it can mean the *wish* for dominance over other ethnic groups. The distinction is blurred, as are combinations of these two types. The one combination most clearly disliked by modern leftists consists of belief in superiority *plus* wish for dominance. But what about ambiguous combinations, such as belief that one's people are objectively superior *plus* striving to liberate inferior peoples or even to make them dominant? Surely noblesse oblige is less objectionable than arrogant aggression? Perhaps Rudyard Kipling was right to extol "the white man's burden" in preference to ruthless exploitation?

There is another possible combination, belief that one's people are inferior *plus* striving for their dominance. Which is more damning, to believe in superiority or attempt to achieve it? It is bad enough that such nuance does not interest those who wield the term "white supremacist" like a club. At the same time, they also refuse to even consider the possibility of non-white supremacism. Those obsessed with white supremacy should reflect on the fact that empires have been rising and falling for four millennia. Most of them were not run by Europeans; some of them ran *over* Europeans.

The possibility that differences in religion, culture and genes underly ethnic differences in wealth, education, and elite representation, has serious consequences. If true, it means that we must learn to live with ethnic and racial inequalities if high rates of diverse immigration continue to outpace assimilation. Because they are not supreme, many whites too must tolerate their inferior status.

Assimilation solves these problems; and assimilation is taking place, both culturally and genetically. Unfortunately, assimilation is not keeping pace with the mass diverse immigration that has been pushed by our liberal-progressive and globalist elites since the 1960s. It is sobering that these elites reject the idea of assimilation, accurately accusing it of being the basis for the White Australia Policy that forged the nation. And they are right to claim that if assimilation is made a priority, then immigration must be returned to its restrictive roots so as to favour Australia's core Euro identity. Instead of assimilation they have installed multiculturalism, the doctrine that minorities should hold onto and perpetuate their identities. It is these very same elites, dominating our universities, schools and media, who insist that ethnic inequality cannot be tolerated. Something has to give, and so far, it is the Anglo majority who are being thrown under the diversity bus. Inequality is claimed to be caused by white racism. This position is hemmed-in by the refusal to countenance the possibility that ethnic groups' long-term relative class position is determined in any way by culture and genes. That position may be irrational; it may be unreasonable; but it *is currently accepted and unchallengeable dogma*. It can also be made to work for a time. If white identity continues to be suppressed, then mass replacement-level immigration is likely to continue until there is no white majority or sizeable minority left to sacrifice.

The reality is that ethnic inequality is here to stay, all the longer if multiculturalism and indiscriminate immigration are continued. Inequality feeds socialism, the expectation that large-scale redistribution will ameliorate inequality. We know this only works to an extent by levelling *down*, not up. It also requires coercion, which would destroy traditional Anglo rule-of-law and civil liberties.

These considerations help explain the rising prominence of accusations of "white supremacy" and other vilifications of Anglos. The taboo against findings of ethnic difference is part of the Anglophobic cage in which we find ourselves.

E. Must be denied the freedom of speech required to promote or pursue the interests of their people, unlike other racial or ethnic groups.

The United Nations Declaration on the Rights of Indigenous Peoples recommends that populations be free to organize to preserve their culture and other interests.[126] There is nothing radical about making this assumption for any non-white or non-Anglo group, whether they be Chinese, Indians, Nigerians, Jews, Palestinians, Malaysians, or any other nationality. All these populations are considered to have a legitimate right to their own nations. The only exceptions to this principle are white, and especially Anglo nations. If the latter express concern about immigration policies, on the grounds that these policies will inevitably consign them to minority status in their own lands, they can lose reputation and employment. They can face baseless accusations of bigotry and intolerance and can even face criminal charges, despite concern about ethnic numbers and wishing to remain the majority being the norm around the world, as discussed in Section 6 below.

An example of the promotion of the selective restriction of free speech comes from Frank Knopfelmacher (1923-1995), who was an academic at Melbourne University. He was a Cold War warrior

---

[126] The UN Declaration on the Rights of Indigenous Peoples was adopted in 2007.
https://www.un.org/development/desa/indigenouspeoples/declaration-on-the-rights-of-indigenous-peoples.html, accessed 4.5.2021.
The government headed by prime minister Julia Gillard subsequently endorsed the Declaration.

who considered Communism to be the main threat to the West. The openness and clarity of his writing reveal the Anglophobic prejudice that had become normal among intellectuals by the 1980s. In a 1984 essay on multiculturalism he began by categorising Anglos as non-ethnics.

Only immigrants from outside the UK and indigenous Australians have ethnicity, he thought. "Non-anglomorph immigrants and Australia-born children from at least one non-anglomorph parent are defined as ethnics . . ." Knopfelmacher saw Anglo identity as having nothing to do with descent or race. Instead, it consisted of "institutions, habits, political structures, and ways of life" derived from the British Isles.

This implied that ethnic identity was not legitimate when felt by Anglos. Knopfelmacher recommended suppressing Anglo ethnicity by introducing criminal penalties for intolerance against Asians. He thought this could be achieved by screening immigrants from the UK to bar those with a history of Anglo advocacy. British immigrants with ethnic attitudes who slipped through the screening should be deported.

Knopfelmacher thought, however, that these harsh measures should only be applied to Anglos. His recommendations were relatively benign for other ethnicities, whose acts of intolerance, he wrote, should not be criminalised. His reason for this distinction was the assertion that Anglo ethnic discrimination undermines national cohesion but the same behaviour by non-Anglos does not.

Knopfelmacher saw the record of multi-ethnic societies in the twentieth century as "catastrophic".

Therefore, he concluded, the "anglomorph cultural hegemony of Australia" should not be tampered with. At the same time, any expression of Anglo ethnicity should be suppressed because "English racism" in Australia threatens "national survival". His argument was that, because Australia is an "anglomorph enclave in an alien sea", assimilation of diverse ethnics is imperative.

He treated the non-discriminatory immigration policy that was creating that diversity, especially permanent mass Asian immigration, as a non-discretionary fact, a force of nature. Somehow, he saw that as compatible with retention of Anglo identity, perhaps because for him Anglos lacked ethnicity.

Unstated in Knopfelmacher's essay was the assumption that Australia lacked a powerful military, and so was forced to rely on the United States to defend it from neighbouring countries. In a 1967 essay Knopfelmacher contrasted Australia's supplicant status to Israel's armed independence, which allowed it to survive in an alien sea.

Military prowess made Israel's ethnic particularism, including restrictive immigration, prudent, unlike Australia. Moreover, Israel was an "impressive and lasting achievement of permanent value" for Jews and for the world (p. 67).

Knopfelmacher implied that Australia could not be a lasting achievement for Anglos despite it being more geographically defensible than Israel due to its large size, distance from potential enemies, and being girt by a vast moat of seas and oceans.

Knopfelmacher was effectively Anglophobic because he singled-out expression of Anglo identity for suppression and Anglo Australia as the vessel of unlimited Asian immigration. This was despite him being relatively moderate, suspicious of multiculturalism, and sympathetic toward aspects of Australia's anglomorph identity.

E-1. Should have their free speech right to express ethnic identity regulated by multicultural agencies such as the Human Rights Commission.

In 2012 Helen Szoke, Australian Race Discrimination Commissioner, stated that Anglo Australians have a special problem with racism not found in other ethnic groups. She claimed that "[p]eople who are part of the majority grouping, the white Anglo-Saxon grouping" deny that their discrimination is racist. Szoke depicted an insensitive Anglo Australia that denies opportunities to Aborigines or immigrants of non-English speaking background. "[T]he white Australia policy is still part of the 'muscle memory' of the more homogenised white Australia."[127] Typical of anti-discrimination advocacy from its earliest days, these disparaging remarks were not balanced by a discussion of non-Anglo networking. Neither did she discuss group interests, for example the cost to the Anglo community of affirmative action for minorities or of infrastructure built for immigrants.

Moreover, Szoke described how her own family had been adversely affected by discrimination in Australia. As she explained it herself: "Here [Australia], our psyche has been scarred . . ."[128] The components of this story sit uncomfortably together – the appointment as race discrimination commissioner of someone with an ethnic and emotional stake in opposing Anglo identity, her categorical criticisms of Anglo Australians, her failure to compare ethnic interests, and her personal

---

[127] Anne Susskind, [Interviews Helen Szoke], *Law Society Journal*, May 2012, pp. 20-22, p. 21.
[128] Anne Susskind, [Interviews Helen Szoke].

ambivalence towards the same ethnic group that she officially condemned. Szoke called for the criminalisation of racial vilification[129].

This anti-Anglo bias was not an aberration. Since its inception, the anti-racism bureaucracy has often been staffed by individuals who have conflicts of interest. They are appointed to administer public policy in an unprejudiced manner, but simultaneously have ethnic or ideological interests in targeting Anglo identity.

White identity has been suppressed by the multicultural apparatus, including the Australian Human Rights Commission, the Racial Discrimination Act 1975, the media and the school system. Since the 1970s multiculturalism of the Anglophobic kind has been official government policy throughout much of the western world, particularly in Anglosphere countries. In a process sometimes called "identity politics", ethnic, religious and cultural groups are welcomed into this fold. They are given access to government resources and funding and are invited to express their group identity, especially as supposed victims of Anglo racism. Politicians seek their votes in exchange for funding, appointments, liberal immigration policies and condemnation of their Anglo critics. Anglos are kept out of this process. Though they pay for multiculturalism's largesse through taxes, their advocates are routinely excluded from the process.

---

[129] *Herald*, 30 Aug. 2012.
Dan Harrison, "Calls for federal law to criminalise racial abuse", *SMH*, 30 Aug. 2012, p. 5.
http://www.smh.com.au/national/calls-for-federal-law-to-criminalise-racial-abuse-20120829-2512p.html.

Political parties do not offer them benefits in immigration or participation in government inquiries. They are excluded from all these perquisites. By and large it is they who are condemned as the common enemy of the multicultural community. This is in stark contrast to the principled multiculturalism publicly advocated by governments.

The history of anti-Anglo multiculturalism is provided by Mark Lopez's ground-breaking *The Origins of Multiculturalism in Australian Politics 1945-1975.* The networks and government committees of the 1960s that gave rise to official multiculturalism were manned by progressives and minority ethnic activists. Anglo advocates were never invited to participate in policy formation. The old Department of Immigration was broken up by the Whitlam government precisely because its officers argued for assimilationist policies that took into account the interests of the majority culture.[130]

Even conservatives such as then Prime Minister John Howard saw fit to consult with the leaders of non-Anglo minorities while ignoring Anglo advocates. For example, Aboriginal leader Noel Pearson reported having had a series of meetings and correspondence with Howard regarding indigenous recognition and reconciliation. "Howard sent me his [2007] speech before he delivered it. Its substance was the subject of various meetings and communications commencing in 2004 and in the lead-up to his Sydney Institute

---

[130] Lopez, M. (2000). *The origins of multiculturalism in Australian politics 1945-1975.* Melbourne, Melbourne University Press.

speech." Pearson also quoted prime minister Scott Morrison as claiming that "I've had numerous meetings myself on this matter" of designing an indigenous Voice to Parliament.[131] Both Howard and Morrison oversaw large scale Third World immigration and refugee intakes without acknowledging the harm this did to Anglo interests. Neither did they consult with leaders of the Anglo community; nor did they attempt to identify such leaders. This contrasts sharply with the care they showed for Aboriginal interests. The displacement of Anglo Australians deserves to become Howard's and Morrison's historical legacy.[132]

Anglo advocates were also excluded from official inquiries into matters of great significance to the historic nation. Examples include the 1988 Fitzgerald Report on immigration, set up by the Hawke Labor government, and the series of committees appointed to develop policy for indigenous recognition, set up by both Labor and Liberal governments. The Expert Panel on Indigenous Constitutional Recognition was appointed by the Gillard Labor government and its follow-up panels were appointed by Coalition

---

[131] Pearson, N. (2021). Recognition and the constitution. *The Weekend Australian.* Sydney, News Corp., 20 March, p. 19. https://www.theaustralian.com.au/inquirer/recognition-of-indigenous-australians-and-the-constitution/news-story/f6cade95b30c85591e287ed74167f225, accessed 28.8.2021.

[132] Wilkinson, P. (2007). *The Howard legacy: Displacement of traditional Australia from the professional and managerial classes.* Essendon, Australia, Independent Australian Publishers.

governments. These panels did not include anyone with a record of advocating Anglo interests, though all other members were either indigenous activists or their non-indigenous supporters.[133]

As the Szoke case illustrates, not all Anglophobia comes from the cultural left, though this has been the powerhouse of anti-white prejudice. As discussed in Section 3a above, its association with the left helps explain multiculturalism's cavalier attitude towards free speech. It is this insensitivity that has tended to suppress Anglo participation in public debates concerning immigration and ethnic affairs.

Minority tribalism has also been an influential source of Anglophobia. As with Leninist ideology, aroused ethnic partisanship by any group often overrides their concern for civil liberties, including free speech. The remainder of this section discusses examples of ethnically motivated Anglophobia that impinge on free speech.

An obvious example of tribal Anglophobia is Islamic jihadi hatred and violence directed against the West, as discussed in Section 7 below. Another example is the

---

[133] Salter, F. K. (2014). "The misguided case for indigenous recognition in the Constitution. Part III: The ethnic bias of the Expert Panel", http://quadrant.org.au/magazine/2014/03/misguided-case-indigenous-recognition-part-iii/. *Quadrant* 58(3): 56-64. (Also in F. Salter, *The Aboriginal question.*)

Salter, F. K. (2015/2018). The new Referendum Council: Gillard's ghost. *The Aboriginal question. Australian racial politics of indigenous recognition and Anglo de-recognition.* F. K. Salter. Sydney, Social Technologies: 171-174.

campaign to impose racial vilification prohibitions. In effect, this was a campaign to silence conservative, and usually Anglo, free speech, on the subject of ethnic affairs. Though often supported by the left, in Australia the campaign has sometimes been led by ethnic minorities and their organisations. For example, Chinese activists and members of the NSW Jewish Board of Deputies significantly influenced the wording of Section 18c, the 1996 amendment to the Racial Discrimination Act (RDA) of 1975.[134] The amendment was passed by the Keating Labor government.

Section 18c has turned the already illiberal Racial Discrimination Act into an instrument of totalitarian domination, because it sets the law against expressions of opinion merely for causing offence, insult or humiliation, all of which are psychological states accessible only to those claiming to be victims. As the Australian Human Rights Commission summarises,

---

[134] Rutland, S. D. and S. Caplan (1998). *With one voice: A history of the New South Wales Jewish Board of Deputies,* Darlinghurst, NSW, Australian Jewish Historical Society, pp. 312-313.

Beginning in 1982, Ian Lacey, honorary secretary of the NSW Jewish Board of Deputies, chaired the NSW government's legal subcommittee authorised to draft an amendment to the Racial Discrimination Act 1975.

See also a report of lobbying of the Keating government in 1994 by the Jewish Community Council of Victoria, the Executive Council of Australian Jewry, and Australia/Israel Publications. Legislation was requested that would ban Holocaust denial:

Kleerekoper, V. and L. Zelazne (1994). Keating gives assurance on vilification law. *Australian Jewish News.* Melbourne, 11 February.

"Section 18c is concerned with [public] acts that offend, insult, humiliate or intimidate because of someone's race or ethnicity."[135] Section 18d allows exemptions if the acts are made in pursuit of academic or artistic expression. These exemptions are not available to most people.

According to the NSW Jewish Board of Deputies, their original goal was to stop the anti-Semitism that was appearing in some Arabic publications.[136] As it transpired, however, Section 18c was mostly used to prosecute Anglos, whether or not they were anti-Semitic. A well-known example involved the journalist Andrew Bolt, who was found guilty of racially vilifying nine individuals of partial Aboriginal descent. Bolt doubted the genuineness of their claimed identity on the grounds that they looked white. He suggested they had emphasised this part of their ancestry to further their careers.

Bolt complained that at his trial he faced a Jewish prosecutor who told the Jewish judge that Bolt was like a neo-Nazi and referred repeatedly to Nazi Germany and the Holocaust. The leading barrister for the plaintiffs even discussed another case he had represented against a Holocaust denier. In a subsequent comment Bolt chided his many Jewish supporters for failing to defend him against what he saw as a scurrilous attack. Bolt concluded that they held their

---

[135] AHRC (2016). Race hate and the RDA. https://humanrights.gov.au/our-work/race-discrimination/projects/race-hate-and-rda#Heading39, accessed 13.8.2021.

[136] Rutland and Caplan, *With one voice*, p. 310.

silence in order to defend Section 18c. He cautioned them that their defence of 18c could be seen as being "largely for the benefit of their own highly articulate and influential community".[137]

In effect, Bolt was making two allegations. Firstly, that the prosecuting lawyer used a slur likely to affect the judge's ethnic sensitivities. And secondly, that Bolt's Jewish supporters failed to defend him because they gave higher priority to defending their ethnic group interests via Section 18c than to defending the principle of free speech. He might also have known that the Jewish barrister and lawyer representing the plaintiffs were working pro bono.[138]

Whatever the merits of the case against Bolt, it appears that the legal team arrayed against him was partly

---

[137] Quoted in Gawenda, M. (2014). Why Andrew Bolt's distress is truly uncomfortable. *The Australian.* 3 April, https://www.theaustralian.com.au/business/business-spectator/news-story/why-andrew-bolts-distress-is-truly-uncomfortable/750b94b0f00eedce7ed31d9331aa2f3d, accessed 10.8.2021.

[138] Quinn, K. (2010). Aborigines sue Bolt over racial writings. *The Age.* Melbourne, Fairfax, 18 September, https://www.theage.com.au/national/victoria/aborigines-sue-bolt-over-racial-writings-20100917-15gk7.html, accessed 19.8.2021 https://www.probonocentre.org.au/news-media-2/apbn-archive/apr-2011/, accessed 12.8.2021. The lawyers working pro bono for the plaintiffs included "senior counsel Ron Merkel QC, Herman Borenstein SC, supported by junior counsel, Claire Harris and Phoebe Knowles and the services of Holding Redlich as solicitor on the record". "Lawyers Joel Zyngier and Natalie Dalpethado from Holding Redlich have put in a lot of the work on the matter recently, working closely with counsel. ... Holding Redlich national pro bono coordinator [was] Linda Rubinstein."

motivated by defensive ethnic sentiment. In other words, the campaign against Andrew Bolt may well have been driven by the strange combination of radical post-ethnic ideology and its exact opposite motivation, ethnic solidarity.

Ethnic defence also appears to have motivated an earlier high-profile litigation relating to Section 18c against Professor Andrew Fraser, a constitutional legal scholar at Macquarie University.[139] The professor had written a letter to a local newspaper criticising the policy that allowed Sudanese immigration which he felt was bound to increase crime. (Statistics on subsequent Sudanese crime are provided below under "C. Violence".)

George Newhouse, a solicitor active in the civil rights arena, organised and led a legal team to lodge a complaint against Fraser on behalf of the Sudanese Darfurian Union. The complaint was lodged with the Human Rights and Equal Opportunity Commission (HREOC), alleging that Fraser had breached Section 18c of the Racial Discrimination Act. The prosecuting team included the president of the NSW Jewish Board of Deputies, the peak Jewish defence agency in New South Wales, that is, the organisation that represented many other Jewish organisations. This would not have

---

[139] Race row professor suspended for 'safety'. *The Sydney Morning Herald*. Fairfax, 30 July 2005, https://www.smh.com.au/national/race-row-professor-suspended-for-safety-20050730-gdls1y.html, accessed 24.8.2021

Fraser, A. (2005). Adventures of an academic pariah. *American Renaissance*. 16: 1-7, https://www.amren.com/news/2020/2011/adventures-of-an-academic-pariah-andrew-fraser/, accessed 2024.2028.2021.

indicated hostility to Anglo identity if Fraser had made anti-Semitic or anti-Israel statements. In such a case, legal action from individuals dedicated to defending their community would have been defensive. In fact, Professor Fraser had no history of making such statements. Instead, Fraser was being attacked for trying to restrict the immigration of a non-Jewish group.

The symbolism could not have been clearer. The leader of a peak Jewish organisation joined with other Jewish lawyers to sue an Anglo professor for raising a legitimate concern of ethnic and national welfare. Like the unprovoked attack on Pauline Hanson,[140] it raises the question, were elements of the organised Jewish community actively opposed to Anglos' legitimate interests of self-defence and remaining the majority in their own country? Or was it a coincidence?

At this point, the editor of the *Deakin* (University) *Law Review* invited Professor Fraser to submit a paper on the matter, providing him with an opportunity to present his arguments in a scholarly manner. The professor did so, and the paper passed peer review. The *Review* was about to publish the paper when Newhouse threatened the university with legal action if it went ahead. He stated to the press: "I put the university on notice that if they repeat the racial vilification, a claim

---

[140] Brunton, R. (1998). Naming rights. *Courier Mail*. Brisbane, News Corporation, 18 July. "Last week the Australia/Israel and Jewish Affairs Council screamed 'Gotcha' to One Nation. ...the council published the names of 2,000 members of Pauline Hanson's party in its magazine, the Australia/Israel Review."

for compensation may be made against the university and the editors that publish or republish this poison."[141] The university's vice chancellor, Sally Walker, informed Fraser that the lawyer representing the Sudanese community had "threatened the University with legal action if it published your article". She claimed to have received legal advice that Fraser's scholarly article "would contravene the Racial Discrimination Act 1975 (Cth) …". Consequently, she overrode the editor and censored Fraser's paper from the *Deakin Law Review*.[142] The legal opinion and the responsible lawyer have never been revealed. The advice is prime facie absurd because Section 18d of the Racial Discrimination Act expressly exempts scholarly works from prosecution.

Newhouse's threat against Deakin University may have reduced Fraser's ability to defend himself under Section 18d, because when Fraser was subsequently found guilty of racial vilification by HREOC, the judgment was made on the grounds that his letter was neither based on academic analysis nor was it a contribution to fair public discussion.

It seems possible that the prosecuting legal team could have been motivated in part by their shared ethnic identity, based on the fact that it was led by Newhouse, who was Jewish, and included a senior lawyer who was also president of the NSW Jewish Board of Deputies,

---

[141] AAP (2005). Legal threat over racist article, *News.com.au*, 14 September.

[142] Walker, Sally (2005). Letter to Associate Professor Andrew Fraser from the Vice-Chancellor of Deakin University, 19 September.

the same agency that had helped compose Section 18c and lobbied to have it legislated. The choice by Newhouse of a team member who was the representative of a Jewish activist group was inconsistent with principled opposition to ethnic particularism. If he opposed ethnic organisation or ethnic nationalism in general, and not just the Anglo kind, why choose a passionate ethnic advocate as an ally?[143] And if he was motivated by opposition to bigotry, why act to prevent Fraser from defending his ideas in a peer-reviewed academic journal?

In 2020 Newhouse did what he had accused Andrew Fraser of doing, by publishing a commentary that lacked scholarly apparatus and contained sweeping defamatory generalisations about an ethnic group, in this case white Australians. He approvingly quoted an Anglophobic statement by Australian author Peter Carey: "All white Australians know that every day [they] are the beneficiaries of genocide". Newhouse went on to make other anti-white accusations, including that the Australian people have a brutal history of dispossessing and colonising indigenous people, and that "the racist attitudes that enabled these mindsets still remain within the fabric of our nation".

---

[143] David D. Knoll A.M., Jewish community service, http://www.davidknoll.com.au/community.html, accessed 21.8.2021.

Knoll, D. D. (2001). Right of return claim avoids Arab responsibility. *The Sydney Morning Herald*. Sydney, Fairfax: 4 January, p. 8, http://www.davidknoll.com.au/files/JCOM/Right%20of%20return%20claim%20avoids%20Arab%20responsibility%20(2001).pdf, accessed 2021.2008.2021.

Such poisonous views may be why he enthusiastically supported the Black Lives Matter movement, notorious for incendiary anti-Anglo and anti-white rhetoric.[144]

The mainstream media portrayed the controversy surrounding Andrew Fraser as involving a clash between Anglo racism and principled universalism. However, the Fraser-Newhouse contest had the hallmarks of a tribal fight. Fraser's most effective antagonists themselves might have been ethnically motivated, despite them wielding the language of universal human rights.

Ethnic motivation might also have been involved in the development of Critical Race Theory (CRT). Recall from Section 4 above that CRT has been adopted as one of the prime tools of leftist radicals. This helps explain why CRT is associated with radical policies and intolerance of free speech wherever it arises. Across the Anglosphere, school children are subjected to this thinly-disguised racism. This ideology masquerading as theory is common in universities and government bureaucracies.

CRT's Marxist roots are well understood, as outlined in Section 4 above. Most CRT ideologues present themselves as opposing white privilege, not the white race. However, some of those academics displayed

---

[144]Newhouse, G. (2020). Australian Aboriginal activists protested against the Nazis. Time for us Jews to return the favor. *Haaretz*. Israel, 7 August, https://www.haaretz.com/world-news/.premium-aboriginal-activists-protested-against-nazis-time-for-us-jews-to-return-the-favor-1.9055020?v=1629463780269, accessed 20.8.2021.

ethnic bias, using whiteness rhetoric to dog-whistle anti-white racism. An example is Noel Ignatiev (1940-2019), a founding figure of Critical Race Theory who famously called for the "abolition of whiteness" and cofounded the journal *Race Traitor* together with the slogan, "Treason to whiteness is loyalty to humanity". Ignatiev did not reach minimum standards of scholarship, such as comparing white ethnic solidarity with that of other ethnicities, including his own.[145]

As someone who grew up Jewish in 1940s and 1950s America, Ignatiev would have had personal experience of the Jewish subculture. He must have known that minority ethnocentrism, endogamous marriage,[146] and ethnic networking, were typically more intense in that minority group than among those of white Gentile Americans. In addition, he surely would have known that Jews and Chinese have higher average incomes than whites. As someone who claimed his research was focused on class, it is inconceivable that Ignatiev was oblivious to the realities of ethnic stratification by socio-economic class in the United States, in which whites do not rate as the highest stratum. Ignatiev claimed to base his belief in white privilege on unequal outcomes and rejected all evidence of group differences in merit. How could he fail to conclude that some minorities were at least as privileged as whites?

---

[145] Ignatiev, N. (1996). *How the Irish became white*. London, Routledge.

[146] See comparison of endogamy by American Jews and mainline Protestants in 1914, in Dutton, E. (2020). *Making sense of race*. Whitefish, MT, Washington Summit Publishers, Pp. 319-321.

It should be noted that in 2007 Ignatiev accused Israel of racist treatment of Palestinians.[147] Did that make him a genuine communist, one who rejected all ethnic and national loyalties? Not if Ignatiev showed what Eric Kaufmann calls "double consciousness". It was common for Anglo idealist liberals in the nineteenth and early twentieth centuries to harbour attachment to their ethnic group, while nevertheless criticising slavery and other gross forms of Anglo racism. They were not truly post-ethnic in line with idealistic liberal principles because they retained some tribal motivation. The same appears to have been true of Ignatiev, because he failed to compare the solidarity and privilege of whites with his own ethnic group. Ignatiev's criticism of Israel was a brief excursion into even-handedness, a rare occasion on which he applied the same communistic standards to that country as he spent his entire academic career applying to white Americans. Whatever else Ignatiev stated about other countries, there was no excuse for failing to identify and compare, in the United States, the wages of whiteness with the wages of Jewishness or Chineseness. Unfortunately, his crude Anglophobia is now widely taught in schools and universities and is influential in the corporate media.

---

[147] The chapter was subsequently removed after protests by Jewish organisations. Ignatiev, N. (2007). Zionism. *Encyclopedia of race and racism*, Macmillan: 240-244. Also see Ignatiev's criticisms of Zionism in his blog, undated but perhaps in mid 2019: Ignatiev, N. (2019-?). My mentioning Israel touches a nerve, https://blog.pmpress.org/2019/09/02/my-mentioning-israel-touches-a-nerve/, accessed 4.11.2021.

An example of the tribal character of Critical Race Theory in the United States is its use by the Anti-Defamation League (ADL), a leading Jewish defence agency. In 2020 the ADL defined racism as the "marginalization and/or oppression of people of color based on a socially constructed racial hierarchy that privileges white people".[148] This implied that only white people can be racist, itself an Anglophobic assertion likely to excuse discrimination against Anglos and other whites. The ADL's statement illustrates how CRT in fact serves prejudice against whites. It is telling that an NGO as sophisticated and richly funded as the ADL adopted a patently Anglophobic definition of racism. It is doubly significant because the ADL has extensive influence, for example on the FBI (according to its director in 2014, James Comey) and on social media giants which it advises regarding who they should ban or curtail.[149] The head of the ADL, Jonathan Greenblatt, boasted about the agency's

---

[148] Brad Jones (2022). Anti-Defamation League changes definition of racism after backlash, https://www.zerohedge.com/political/anti-defamation-league-changes-definition-racism-after-backlash, 4 February 2022.

[149] Comey, J. B. (2014). *The FBI and the ADL: Working towards a world without hate* [transcript of speech]. Federal Bureau of Investigation, 28 April, https://www.fbi.gov/news/speeches/the-fbi-and-the-adl-working-toward-a-world-without-hate, accessed 12.3.2019.

Anti-Defamation League (2017). Facebook, Google, Microsoft, Twitter, and ADL announce lab to engineer new solutions to stop cyberhate, *ADL*, 10 October, https://www.adl.org/news/press-releases/facebook-google-microsoft-twitter-and-adl-announce-lab-to-engineer-new?mod=722, accessed 19.2.2022. Google owns YouTube.

influence before and after Twitter was purchased by free-speech advocate Elon Musk in 2022:

> So literally, we opened a centre in Silicon Valley back in 2017. And the woman who runs it, she's an ex-Facebook executive. I have software engineers and data scientists working at ADL. We are monitoring all this stuff and we're working with all the platforms by the way – Google and YouTube and Meta and Twitter and Reddit and Steam and Amazon and all these companies. From like Apple to Zoom we work with all of them, okay? That's relevant because we work with Twitter now since it was founded. We worked with the old regime and [we're] working with the new regime.[150]

These examples of Jewish activism against Anglo interests involve an intense level of motivation. The individuals and organisations concerned devoted significant resources to these attacks. This begs the question of why? What was the motivating factor which drove these protagonists. This behaviour is puzzling because Jews are safer and more comfortable in the Anglosphere than anywhere else in modern history, apart from Israel perhaps. They enjoy absolute equality in opportunity and levels of anti-Semitism are vanishingly low. Almost the same number of Jews

---

[150] Greenblatt, J. (2022). Jonathan Greenblatt on combatting anti-Semitism, anti-black racism, Kanye West, Kyrie Irving and more, *Breakfast Club Power 105.1 FM*, 8 December. https://www.youtube.com/watch?v=wVXcIcIBtTU&t=3643s, accessed 10.12.2022.

choose to live in North America as in Israel, their ancient homeland.

It is important to understand what drives Jewish Anglophobia because, as we have seen, Jewish organisations have often played a leading role in advancing multiculturalism. In Britain, for example, the late Lord Jonathan Sacks, when Chief Rabbi of Orthodox synagogues in Great Britain, stated that the Jewish community had pioneered identity politics, though he regretted that the process had gotten out of hand after being taken up by numerous other groups.[151] In Europe some Jews see themselves as having a leading role in managing the transformation of homogeneous nations such as Sweden, Germany and France. For example, Barbara Spectre, an academic who helped found the European Institute of Jewish Studies in Sweden, stated in 2011:

> I think we are going to be part of the throes of that [multicultural] transformation. Europe is not going to be monolithic societies that they once were in the twentieth century. Jews are going to be in the centre of that. It's a huge transformation for Europe to make. They are now going into a multicultural mode and Jews will be resented because of our leading role. But without that

---

[151] Associated Press (2007). Britain's top rabbi warns against multiculturalism, 20 October 20.

Also: (2013). Britain's chief rabbi: Multiculturalism threatens liberal democracy, *Jerusalem Post*, 20 October, https://www.jpost.com/jewish-world/jewish-news/britains-chief-rabbi-multiculturalism-threatens-liberal-democracy, accessed 28.10.2022.

leading role and without that transformation Europe will not survive.[152]

Whether or not Sacks' and Spectre's claim to stewardship is true, they as least saw themselves as leading the multicultural movement. This self-perception has a marked dimension of ethnic identity, and so cannot be attributed solely to universalist values.

In Australia, Jewish organisations sometimes act as de facto peak bodies for the multicultural sector as a whole, rallying, organising, coordinating, and supporting the actions of other minority advocates. Consider the following cases.

An example is the NSW Jewish Board of Deputies, a peak body that represents 166 Jewish organisations in the state of New South Wales in 2022,[153] As we have seen, in the 1990s the JBD was involved in formulating Section 18C of the Racial Discrimination Act. We have also discussed how, in 2006, the president of the organisation was a member of the legal team representing the Sudanese Darfurian Union in its complaint, based on Section 18C, against Professor Andrew Fraser's warning about high Sudanese crime levels.

---

[152] Spectre, Barbara Lerner (2011). Jews will play a leading role in multicultural Europe says Jewish researcher, IBA News Television,
https://www.youtube.com/watch?v=53A5AJoRxF0,
accessed 5 November 2022.

[153] New South Wales Jewish Board of Deputies (2022). Communal directory, https://www.nswjbd.org/communal-directory-public/, accessed 19.5.2022.

In the 1960s, Walter Lippmann, a former president of the Victorian Jewish Board of Deputies, was an effective early promoter of multiculturalism in Australia. In his history of that ideology, Mark Lopez concludes that Lippmann was the preeminent early promoter.[154]

Jewish organisations have also played a leading role in building the Aboriginal protest movement. In 2011 then prime minister Julia Gillard appointed Mark Leibler as co-chair of the Expert Panel on Constitutional Recognition of Indigenous Australians. Leibler published the magazine *Australia/Israel Review* which doxed 2,000 One Nation members and had been active in Jewish communal affairs. He had also been active in supporting the indigenous movement. Leibler accepted Gillard's appointment and co-chaired the Panel of around 20 indigenous advocates and white supporters. He helped manage the committee's deliberations on how best to amend the Constitution, a document important for all Australians. The committee did not include a single advocate for Anglo Australia, the majority and founding ethny.[155]

---

[154] Lopez, M. (2000). *The origins of multiculturalism in Australian politics 1945-1975*. Melbourne, Melbourne University Press.

Markus, A. (2017). Lippman, Walter Max (1919-1993), Australian Dictionary of Biography, National Centre of Biography, Australian National University, https://adb.anu.edu.au/biography/lippmann-walter-max-18257, accessed 18.5.2022.

[155] Salter, F. K. (2018). *The Aboriginal question: Australian racial politics of indigenous recognition and Anglo de-recognition. Collected essays II*, Social Technologies.

Also reported earlier was the 2011 prosecution of Andrew Bolt under Section 18C. The Aboriginal complainants were represented by a Jewish lawyer working pro bono.[156]

Later in this section we describe how, in 2014, Jewish leaders organised several ethnic communities to lobby against plans to reform Section 18C by the government of Tony Abbott.

Jewish organisations continue to reach out to help coordinate and support otherwise poorly organised ethnic groups. A recent example involves the rapidly growing African population in Australia. In June 2021 the NSW Jewish Board of Deputies and the African Australian Advocacy Centre – the AAAC – held an inaugural friendship dinner. The AAAC is a peak body formed in 2019 to represent all African communities in Australia.[157]

The rationale for this cooperation was that the Jewish and African communities shared a common negative experience in Australia: "African communities and Jewish communities in Australia have shared experiences of racism and prejudice. This reinforces the importance of making connections between the two

---

[156] Quinn, K. (2010). Aborigines sue Bolt over racial writings. *The Age*. Melbourne, Fairfax, 18 September, https://www.theage.com.au/national/victoria/aborigines-sue-bolt-over-racial-writings-20100917-15gk7.html, accessed 19.8.2021.

[157] Website of the African Australian Advocacy Centre, https://africanaustralianadvocacy.org.au/about, accessed 19.5.2022.

communities to overcome societal barriers caused by negative stigma."[158]

The Jewish Board of Deputies has already opened doors for the AAAC by ushering it into a coalition group, "Keep NSW Safe". The coalition has 40 member organisations and prominent individuals, but no Anglo bodies. The NSW Jewish Board of Deputies initiated Keep NSW Safe in 2016, providing its first spokesman. This was a clear example of a Jewish organisation carrying out leadership functions for the multicultural community as a whole.[159] The mission of Keep NSW Safe, is to amend Section 20d of the NSW Anti-Discrimination Act to "make incitement to violence" "on the basis of race, religion, gender, sexuality and a number of other categories a crime".[160] Of course incitement to violence has been illegal for a long time in Australia, indicating that the actual goal of the organisation may be to expand the definition of "incite" to facilitate prosecution and apply criminal penalties to things which would currently be protected as free speech.

The foregoing are examples of Jewish organisations carrying out leadership functions for the multicultural community as a whole. As far as we are aware, no other

---

[158] Inaugural friendship dinner for African and Jewish leaders [10 June 2021], AAAC & Jewish Community Dinner Report, https://img1.wsimg.com/blobby/go/ddd70bca-c2d9-436e-8e38-91fa560c87ea/Inaugural%20Friendship%20Dinner%20for%20Afri can%20and%20Je.pdf, accessed 19.5.2022.

[159] Keep Australia Safe – A success story, https://www.keepnswsafe.com/, accessed 19.5.2022.

[160] Inaugural friendship dinner for African and Jewish leaders [June 2021].

ethnic organisations have acted as peak multicultural bodies. These examples of the organised Jewish community's leadership of multiculturalism therefore make it important to understand what motivates instances of Jewish Anglophobia.

It is difficult, of course, to determine the motivation of an entire racial/religious group. Not all members of a group will share identical reasons for particular beliefs or actions. One clue, however, was given in a statement made by a Jewish advocate, Miriam Faine.

At that time, Faine was a Victorian teacher and editor of the Jewish community journal, *Australian Jewish Democrat*. She made the following remarks in a 1992 article, in which she discussed how multiculturalism and immigration policy affect Australian Jews, and vice versa. She began by condemning Australia's formal and informal acknowledgment of its Anglo roots.

> "Australia ... even today, clearly values one of its immigrant cultures and heritages (the British Anglo-Saxon) above all the others."[161]

Instead, Faine stated, the country should see itself as a collection of equally valuable migrant groups. This is a sensible approach from the perspective of a member of a minority ethno-religious group looking to increase its relative power and prestige. She asserted that immigration should favour minority ethnic groups, in order to build up their ethnic identity. In her article, she

---

[161] Faine, Miriam (1992). The Jewish community and the immigration debate. *Australian Jewish Democrat: A journal of independent Jewish thought* (Winter): 9-10, p. 10.

stated that, "A successful on-going immigration policy would take as its first premise the need to support the ethnic identity of those already settled here and to maintain and encourage the diversity within the community."[162]

Faine accused assimilationist, pre-multicultural governments, i.e., every single one prior to the 1970s, of being racist. In support she quoted the Lyons government of the 1930s. They had described German Jews seeking to immigrate as difficult to assimilate. Faine's response was to recommend a minority ethnic coalition to defeat the Anglo community. She wrote: "Therefore we should make it our business to strike common cause with other non-Anglo groups to promote a multi-cultural Australia." The strategy was not new, because multiculturalism was from its beginning a form of cultural and demographic warfare against Anglo Australia. What was new about Faine's words, was their honesty.

Faine saw her approach as a diaspora strategy, as opposed to one of migrating to Israel. "With the demise of Zionism ... ...", she wrote, "it is precisely such a multi-cultural society which would give space for Australian Jews to fulfil their hopes for the continuation of the community. The strengthening of multi-cultural or diverse Australia is also our most effective insurance policy against anti-Semitism. The day Australia has a Chinese Australian Governor-General I would feel more confident of my freedom to live as a Jewish Australian."

---

[162] Faine, ibid.

Already at that time, Faine saw her anti-Anglo strategy being implemented. She explained that "[i]t is in our own interests as Jews to advocate on immigration and ethnic issues, as Jews in the wider community, and we should welcome the initiative of the ECAJ [Executive Council of Australian Jewry] and Orthodox and Reform rabbinate in supporting the Cambodians and hope it continues."[163] The ECAJ was and is the peak body representing Jewish organisations across Australia. Faine was praising the organisation for lobbying on behalf of Cambodian refugees around 1992. This action was also being supported by religious Jewish bodies. Whatever the motives of these organisations, Faine made her own motives very clear. She saw non-white refugees as allies in breaking down Anglo influence.

Faine's hate-filled words give us a window into explicit multicultural strategising. She did not express vague unconscious implicit prejudice. This was someone intent on group domination and replacement, in a very conscious and deliberate targeting of Anglo Australia. The motivation for this behaviour sprang from an extremely pessimistic assessment of Anglo behaviour and history as inherently ethnocentric and anti-Semitic. This pessimism might have been a projection of Faine's own ethnocentrism and group defensiveness, both of which she expressed with unusual intensity.

We cannot say for sure whether Faine's sentiments were unusual within the Jewish community. Perhaps

---

[163] Faine, ibid.

her views were roundly condemned at the time by Jewish leaders and we missed those articles. However, a year after her article appeared, a mainstream Jewish journal, *The Australian Jewish News*, reviewed the *Australian Jewish Democrat*. The reviewer found the journal to offer a perspective which was not fundamentally out of step with the Jewish mainstream. He reported that instead of being aligned with religious or Zionist Jews, the journal adopted a mix of ethnic and radical perspectives supporting "the preservation of Jewish life, a wide-ranging pluralism, social justice, peace, *Tikkun Olam*, interaction with Australian society", which the reviewer judged to be "legitimate Jewish expression" because they are "never offensive to, or undermining of, Jewish interests". In other words, though the *Australian Jewish Democrat* was secular and occasionally critical of Israel, it presented an ethnically loyal way of examining issues that affected the Jewish people.[164] The reviewer was reassuring his readers that though the *AJD* was progressive, it was supportive of the diaspora way of life, even though it was different from the traditional religious approach of Judaism and the nationalist approach of Zionism.

Although Faine explained that she would not feel safe as a Jewish person in Australia until the country had a Chinese person acting as Governor General, she did

---

[164] Liberman, Serge (1993). People of the Book: *The Australian Jewish Democrat*, *The Australian Jewish News*, Sydney Edition, 29 October, p. 9.
https://trove.nla.gov.au/newspaper/article/261623727, accessed 18.2.2022.

not express any special attachment to China or to the Chinese. Therefore, it seems likely that the term "Chinese" meant any non-Anglo or non-European.

The Governor General is the Australian head of state, so Faine was expressing a preference for Anglos to be replaced in positions of power. Apparently, she saw Anglos as posing the major threat of anti-Semitism. Therefore, she recommended increasing diversity which, as discussed, is often a code word for reducing the proportion of Anglos or whites.

Once these steps had been taken, once the hostile ethnic group had been reduced in demography and power, only then would Ms Faine feel safe. But why would she not feel safe in a country like Australia which has no significant history of anti-Semitism? There has never been a serious political party with anti-Jewish policies in its platform. There has never been a political leader who has verbally attacked Jews. During the First World War, Australians played a large role in liberating Palestine, and thus Israel's future territory, from the Ottoman Empire. Australia was an early supporter of Israel after its declaration of independence in 1948 and has maintained a friendly posture since then. What would cause Ms Faine to feel so threatened by Anglos? Surely it was not the mere possibility of anti-Semitic politics arising? Such thinking would justify attacking in many directions, but Ms Faine singled out Anglos. A cause is hard to imagine. Fear is a strong emotion, but whatever Ms Faine was afraid of, she was acting on that fear by wishing for the disempowerment of white Anglo Christians. It is hard to know if this fear, and the reaction to it, are widespread in the Jewish community. If so, then it could be one reason for the examples given above of strong Jewish support for non-white mass immigration into white and Anglo countries. As well as being irrational, however, the wish to strip Anglos of power and swamp them demographically in their own nations is an unambiguous act of Anglophobia.

Jewish Anglophobia is sometimes understandable. Anti-Semitism is real and although its frequency has been low among Anglos for a long time, it is reasonable for Jews to be resentful when it does occur. Given their history of persecution, it is also understandable that they remain alert. In such circumstances it is reasonable that Jews organise to oppose the defamation of their people and emphasise disabilities suffered by them. Examples of recent Anglo anti-Semitism include the modern neo-Nazi movement. This movement is sometimes violent but is tiny and lacks organisation, funding, patronage and any semblance of mainstream acceptance. Historical examples are also relevant. During the 1930s the British Fascists under Sir Oswald Mosely were anti-Semitic. They had counterparts in the United States. Further back, Jews not converted to Christianity were prevented from serving in the British Parliament until 1858. In 1290 King Edward I of England expelled the Jewish community.

For historical reasons Jews, especially secular Jews, are typically on the political left and are often very sensitive to any sign of Gentile ethnic solidarity. For reasons of individual merit they are also overrepresented in the professions, including in academe. It is likely that these factors taken together helped cause the examples of Anglophobia described above. Though Anglophobia is evident in some Jewish organisations, it does not define them. Those bodies mostly perform welfare and legitimate representative functions. The voluntary labour and philanthropy upon which these organisations rest spring from prosocial motivations, not Anglophobia.

Jews have flourished in Anglosphere nations due, in part, to the rule of law. Benjamin Disraeli served as British prime minister as early as 1868. Sir Isaac Isaacs was an early governor general of Australia. Anti-Semitism has never been entrenched in Anglo societies as it has been in Eastern Europe or the Middle East. Yet the cases reviewed above indicate unprovoked hostility to Anglo Australia. In such circumstances, attempting to undermine or disempower an ethnic group within its own nation has no moral basis. This is especially true in a robust, advanced, and fully functioning liberal democracy.

Irish Catholics have also been known to display ethnically motivated Anglophobia in Australia and elsewhere. Some individuals have continued the centuries-long conflict between England and Ireland. Anglo prejudice against Irish-Catholics has been analysed in numerous scholarly and popular texts, while the reverse hostility has received less attention.[165]

---

[165] For example, see the Irish-centric review article: Marley, L. (2019). The history of the Irish in Australia: Racial profiling down under. *The Irish Times*. 2 February,

If Anglophobia is defined as any attack on the British, then 18th and 19th century rebellions against British occupation of Ireland might be categorised as such. Surely that would be an error. Aggression motivated by the aspiration for ethnic or religious defence or for national independence is not Anglophobic in any meaningful way. In that circumstance, neither is hatred of British symbols linked to oppression.

For this reason, Irish fractiousness in early Australian and American history cannot be simply categorised as Anglophobic, though naturally some ethnic hatred would have been involved on both sides. By 1800 Irish rebels were being transported to Australia as a means of suppressing the Irish nationalist movement. These Irish convicts sought to return to Ireland to continue the fight against British occupation. In 1804 about 400 mainly Irish convicts rose up in armed revolt in what is known as the Castle Hill Rebellion. They were put down by the NSW Corps.[166] In 1868 Irish rebelliousness spilled over again in Sydney when an Irishman wounded Prince Alfred, Queen Victoria's son, in a failed assassination attempt.

By 1921 Ireland had gained independence from Britain. In addition, by that date Irish immigrant communities in Australia and the United States were well on their way to economic and political integration.

---

https://www.irishtimes.com/culture/books/a-new-history-of-the-irish-in-australia-racial-profiling-down-under-1.3768249, accessed 19.10.2021.

[166] Castle Hill Rising, *Encyclopedia Britannica*.
https://www.britannica.com/event/Castle-Hill-Rising, accessed 4.11.2021.

These events make it less plausible to categorise later examples of anti-Anglo behaviour as defensive. Irish-Australian hostility towards Anglo-Australia was at its most popular shortly before Irish independence. During the First World War, Prime minister Billy Hughes sought to introduce conscription in order to maintain Australia's contribution to the Anglo-French alliance in the face of heavy casualties. Two referenda were called by Hughes, in 1916 and 1917. These were his attempts to give conscription powers to the Commonwealth. While most British-descended Australians voted for conscription, most Irish-Catholics voted against it. Doctor Daniel Mannix, an Irish patriot who was appointed Catholic Archbishop of Melbourne, urged his parishioners to oppose conscription. Both referenda were defeated, partly due to Mannix's opposition.

Whilst many of those who followed Mannix's voting advice were likely moved, in part, by Anglophobia, there were other powerful motivations. The War had inflicted grievous wounds on Australia, notably at Gallipoli in 1915. The country would lose 60,000 young men during the War, out of a population of fewer than 5 million. So many men enlisted that about 39 percent of the adult male population served in the armed forces between 1914 and 1919.[167]

Minority ethnic activists often adopt radical ideological positions to present themselves as victims and

---

[167] Enlistment statistics, First World War. *Australian War Memorial*, https://www.awm.gov.au/articles/encyclopedia/enlistment/ww1, accessed 8.11.2021.

undermine the legitimacy of their majority opponents. In Australia this tendency has been expressed by some politicians and intellectuals of Irish descent, including those who have lost the Catholic faith. Ideological vehicles of Irish Anglophobia include multiculturalism and republican nationalism, which attempts to strip away connections to Britain, including flag and monarchy.

Persistent Irish Anglophobia can be nastier. Thomas Keneally, in his book, *The Chant of Jimmie Blacksmith* (1972), sought to evoke readers' sympathetic understanding of the racially-motivated murder of nine Anglo men, women and children by an embittered Aboriginal man, based loosely on a rampage by Jimmy Governor, an historical figure from 1901. Keneally and Fred Schepisi, the director of the film adaptation of Keneally's book, used the opportunity to not only exculpate racially-motivated violence, but to vilify the Methodist Church and its missionaries (discussed further in section 7 below). The book was nominated for a Booker Prize in 1972. Keneally has never apologised for his book nor criticised Schepisi's anti-Christian film.

Greg Sheridan, senior editor at *The Australian* newspaper, is another example of Irish Catholic identity coinciding with bitterness towards Anglo Australia decades after the conflict between Britain and Ireland was resolved. Though born and raised in Sydney, he was immersed in Irish nationalism and the historical grudge it can engender. At his father's knee he learnt of 800 years of British persecution.[168] "I was a republican kid ..." he wrote, "so I refused point-blank during my school years ever to stand for God Save the Queen or in any other way to acknowledge English sovereignty over Australia."[169]

Later in life Sheridan conceded that English culture had some good points, while maintaining enmity against British-Australian identity and pride. As a journalist writing for *The Australian* newspaper in the 1970s, he was critical of the British connection and became a committed multiculturalist. He promoted Asian immigration and argued that Australia's future lay in close integration with Asia. He supported demographic transformation through "Asianisation", and the globalisation and deindustrialisation of the Australian economy through removal of industry protection. He was enthusiastic about the end of Anglo Australia. "I am a constant champion when I am in Asia", he wrote, "for Australia and for the great success of Asian immigration and the many other things which make this a lovely, honey-coloured society."[170]

Sheridan's attitude began to change when he and his family suffered from Islamic aggression in their

---

[168] Sheridan, G. (2014). A brave move for Scotland. *The Weekend Australian.* Sydney, News Corp, 6-7 January.

[169] Sheridan, G. (1988). Why Australia must forget foreign symbols. *The Weekend Australian.* Sydney, News Corp, 30-31 January.

[170] Sheridan, G. (1995). *Living with dragons: Australia confronts its Asian destiny.* St Leonards, NSW, Allen & Unwin with Mobil Oil Australia, p. 171.

Sydney suburb. By 2011 Sheridan called into question decades of multiculturalist activism in an article titled "How I Lost Faith in Multiculturalism", though he did not clearly identify diversity as the core problem.[171] In a subsequent article he expressed polite regret at how the policies he had promoted resulted in the cultural genocide of Anglo Australia.[172] "Almost from the first words I wrote for public consumption I have strongly supported this policy [Asian immigration]. ... It has resulted, incidentally, in a kind of benign cultural genocide. The old race of 'Austral-Britons' is gone forever." Sheridan undermined his already lukewarm expression of regret by qualifying the cultural genocide as "benign". He explicitly supported the displacement of Anglo Australia: "The old Austral-Britons have been supplanted by a much more diverse range of ethnic and cultural backgrounds. I don't feel at all unhappy about that ..."

Sheridan has maintained the same hostility towards Anglo identity wherever it exists. In 2015 he criticised Nigel Farage's UKIP because he thought it represented English nationalism.[173] Also in 2015 Sheridan managed to combine praise for Australia's ethnic transformation with acceptance of India's efforts to remain majority Hindu through control of

---

[171] Sheridan, G. (2011). How I lost faith in multiculturalism. *The Australian*, 2 April. Sydney, News Limited.

[172] Sheridan, G. (2014). Constitutional change will divide not unite the nation. *The Australian*. Sydney, News Limited, 20 September.

[173] Sheridan, Greg. (2015). Pity centrists, beware the nationalists and praise Australia's good friend. *The Australian*. Sydney, News Corporation, 14 May.

immigration. He described India's policy without criticism, sarcasm, or irony. And that is as it should be, given how normal such a policy is throughout the non-western world today and in the West prior to the 1960s.[174] Sheridan admitted the normalcy of ethnic selectiveness in choosing immigrants, at least for non-western societies. He praised the cultural continuity this makes possible, writing of Indian culture "stretching back across the centuries". He offered similar remarks about China, also in a matter-of-fact way.[175]

If Sheridan applied the same standards to India and China that he applies to Australia, he would have to believe that Hindus and Han Chinese could become minorities in their own countries without losing anything precious, so long as the transformation was peaceful. Sheridan did not articulate such a perverse standard, which speaks well of his Christianity and common sense. Unfortunately, he has not extended this benevolence to Australia or other Anglosphere nations.

There is an extraordinary contradiction between Sheridan's conservatism on many issues and his Anglophobia. On the conservative side he evinces an essentially neoconservative set of policies – strong defence and alliances with other western societies,

---

[174] Sheridan, Greg. (2015). Boatpeople crisis a global phenomenon. *The Weekend Australian*. Sydney, Newscorp, 16-17 May, p. 17.
[175] Sheridan, G. (2015). A geeks' paradise in Mysore is among the most magnificent temples of a forward-looking India. *The Weekend Australian*. Sydney, News Corp, 16-17 May, p. 24.

juxtaposed with a cavalier, even subversive, attitude towards the West's demographic interests. This contradiction embroils his abiding Catholicism, because that religion is compatible with his conservative side but not his attitude to national identity. Indeed, Sheridan's ruthless treatment of white Australia is un-Christian.

No Catholic, no Christian, of any seriousness who was aware of first principles would agree that cultural genocide can ever be "benign". This Orwellian language is the opposite of Christian grace and charity. It resembles a mask for ethnic hatred.

Saint Thomas Aquinas (1225-1274), the great Catholic philosopher, the renowned "Doctor of the Church", was explicit in how nations should treat immigrants according to biblical principles. He cited scriptures that acknowledged peaceful and hostile relations with foreigners.[176] He discerned in the Old Testament types of peaceful treatment of visitors – charity, respect and courtesy – but only if they are compatible with the receiving nation. Saint Thomas put the welfare of the host nation first, its unity and commonwealth. There is no obligation to accept all comers. If visitors seek to remain, their complete acceptance should await a trial period of two or three generations, as recommended by

---

[176] Aquinas, Saint Thomas (1947). *Summa Theologica*, https://www.sacred-texts.com/chr/aquinas/summa/sum243.htm, accessed 12.11.2021. "Man's relations with foreigners are twofold: peaceful, and hostile: and in directing both kinds of relation the Law contained suitable precepts."

Aristotle.[177] To be accepted permanently, immigrants should become part of the society and bear no hostile intentions towards it. Saint Thomas noted that Ancient Israel was more likely to accept immigrants who were similar to the Jews.[178]

Saint Thomas's stipulation of a trial period implies that if a group of immigrants is proving injurious to the nation, they should be repatriated, even if that means expelling their great grandchildren. The *Genesis* story of the Tower of Babel also fits Saint Thomas's thesis. God punished the people who had displeased Him by making them speak different languages, resulting in social chaos and collapse. Modern social research confirms that the most stable and peaceful societies are ethnically homogenous, a phenomenon discussed earlier in the section headed "Sociological Dimensions of Racism".[179] Homogeneity is incompatible with

---

[177] Aquinas, *Summa Theologica.* "Thirdly, when any foreigners wished to be admitted entirely to their fellowship and mode of worship. With regard to these a certain order was observed. For they were not at once admitted to citizenship: just as it was law with some nations that no one was deemed a citizen except after two or three generations, as the Philosopher says (Polit. iii, 1)."

[178] Aquinas, *Summa Theologica.* "Nevertheless it was possible by dispensation for a man to be admitted to citizenship on account of some act of virtue: thus it is related (Judith 14:6) that Achior, the captain of the children of Ammon, 'was joined to the people of Israel, with all the succession of his kindred.'"

[179] Salter, F. K., Ed. (2004). *Welfare, ethnicity, & altruism: New data & evolutionary theory*. London, Frank Cass.

Putnam, R. D. (2007). E Pluribus Unum: Diversity and community in the twenty-first century. The 2006 Johan

indiscriminate mass immigration. It can only be sustained by regulating immigration and promoting assimilation.

The ancient Middle East was harsh, and the liberality of policies was constrained by an almost subsistence economy and endemic warfare. Though times have changed, it can never be argued that the Christian tradition evaluates immigrant policy only through the lens of minority interests and rates host societies as expendable.

Sheridan has formed part of a broader institutional Anglophobia. For much of his career he has been employed by *The Australian* newspaper, part of the media empire controlled by Rupert Murdoch. The newspaper has been Murdoch's loss-making show pony since he founded it in 1964. Murdoch's News Corporation has become more diverse in its commentary than its leftist rivals. However, as discussed further in Section 5b, its spectrum of views has rarely if ever included a champion of Anglo Australian identity or interests. Sheridan's promotion of replacement immigration has not been balanced by different views. There have been no long-term journalists who openly and proudly identified with Anglo-Australians and advocated their interests.

Skytte Prize lecture. *Scandinavian Political Studies* 30: 137-174.

Vanhanen, T. (2012). *Ethnic conflicts: Their biological roots in ethnic nepotism*. London, Ulster Institute for Social Research.

Sheridan has never felt moved to object to this suppression of free speech.

The censorship of Anglo-loyalist voices in the Murdoch media may have involved more than the usual multi-cultural coalition of minority and radical motivations. Corporate ideology might also have played a role, from the desire to increase population and thus profits. After all, those responsible for denying media platforms to Anglo advocates were in the senior ranks of News Corporation. In 2014 Rupert Murdoch celebrated the 50th anniversary of *The Australian*. In his Sydney speech he urged Australians to keep the immigration doors open wide.[180] This was at a time when the country was drowning in a government-sponsored flood of immigration at the rate of about one percent of the Australian population arriving every year. That is the equivalent of the United States receiving over three million migrants annually or China receiving 14 million.

The reduction of Australia's enviable homogeneity and low population density has been a victory for corporate interests who want a Big Australia of 100 million. They are willing to accomplish that goal at any cost to free speech, the environment and social harmony.

The case of Greg Sheridan shows that elitist anti-white bigotry is not a recent product of Big Tech and social media. It has been a prominent feature of mainstream

---

[180] Murdoch, R. (2014). Speech at the Gala Dinner celebrating the 50th anniversary of *The Australian* newspaper, https://australianpolitics.com/2014/07/15/murdoch-abbott-speeches-the-australian-50th.html, accessed 15 July 2021.

academia and the media since the 1960s at the latest. Thomas Sowell, a senior American social analyst, identifies the universities as the main long-term source of divisive racial sentiment. He notes that Barack Obama, a Harvard-educated lawyer, accepted the sermons of his Chicago pastor, Jeremiah Wright, despite the latter being a "ranting racist" who condemned white America. In his 2010 book *Dismantling America*, Sowell described how the Obama administration was pulling down marriage, culture and self government, bringing America closer to civilisational collapse.[181]

The only change in recent years is the openness of the hatred expressed by Marxist organisations such as Black Lives Matter and ideologies such as Critical Race Theory. Australia's ongoing demographic transformation cannot be understood without realising its elite origins.

Through a process of elimination, it is reasonable to link Sheridan's callousness towards Anglo Australia with his tribal identity. It cannot be that his views on immigration have been based on left-liberal principles, because he has openly promoted Asian immigration to Australia, a discriminatory goal, accepted the main-stream media's censorship of pro-restrictionist views, failed to demand democratic process, while accepting discrimination in the immigration policies of Asian nations. There is no excuse for such obstinate resentment from someone who shares so much of

---

[181] Sowell, Thomas (2010). Dismantling America, Hoover Institution, https://youtu.be/5SDLBqIubCs, accessed 19.2.2021, 6:15 minutes.

Anglo Australia's identity, who was fully accepted into Australian society, and was able to reach the top of his field in the same society that for most of his career he assiduously attempted to destroy.

Examples of Anglophobia can be found among Irish Catholics, but that sentiment has not been general or inevitable. An example is Arthur Calwell (1896-1973), a leading light of the Labor Party. Calwell advocated shaping immigration policy to maintain racial homogeneity. As immigration minister in the Chifley Labor Government, he put in place the post-War immigration policy that brought millions from Europe. Calwell was born and raised in Australia and was a staunch Catholic. He was also a supporter of Irish independence. In his youth Calwell protested against the British occupation of Ireland. He supported Archbishop Mannix and considered him a gift to Australia as well as a loyal Irishman. At the same time, he was unhappy that Mannix took the side of the anti-Communist Democratic Labour Party when it split with Calwell's Labor Party in the 1950s, keeping the latter out of office for a generation. Calwell saw no contradiction between his love of Catholic Ireland and loyalty to white Australia.[182]

Irish Catholic Anglophobia has largely faded, though residual traces remain. Most Australians of Irish descent count themselves as part of the mainstream. The partisanship and aggression shown by a few writers

---

[182] Calwell, Arthur A. (1978/1972). *Be just and fear not.* Adelaide, Rigby.

and politicians have mostly been overwhelmed by shared identity and equal rights.

The same process of reconciliation is evident in other peoples whose Anglophobia-like behaviour was forced upon them by British colonialism. Australian Aborigines are an important example. During the century of British colonisation, no reasonable person could blame the indigenous inhabitants for resisting, sometimes with violence. Their way of life was being transformed. Many were being pushed off their ancient homelands. From their perspective the British annexation did have invasion-like characteristics, and armed resistance was understandable. The excuse does not extend to massacres of settler families, which did occur on the frontier. The modern Aboriginal rights movement operates in different circumstances. It is reasonable for the nation to expect loyalty from citizens with indigenous ancestry because the days of colonisation are long gone and been replaced by equal, and from 2020 superior, ethnically-privileged, citizen-ship rights.[183] Aborigines and Torres Strait Islanders receive generous benefits, from education to health care. They are counted as part of the nation. They have been granted large concessions in the form of land rights. Modern Australia encourages the expression of indigenous identity, including advocacy of community interests. There is no excuse for the Aboriginal move-ment to cooperate with those who hate Anglo

---

[183] BBC News (2020). Aboriginal Australians born overseas cannot be deported, court rules, 11 February, https://www.bbc.com/news/world-australia-51455256, accessed 16.11.2021.

Australia, including elements of the multicultural establishment.

The trial of Andrew Bolt and another prosecution of Anglo students in Brisbane, led to a popular backlash and a promise by Liberal leader Tony Abbott to reform Section 18c. When in 2013 Abbott became prime minister and tried to enact this policy, he was stopped by a group of minority advocates organised by Jewish leaders, according to senior journalist Michael Gawenda'. The group included representatives of the **indigenous, Greek, Chinese, Arab, Armenian, and Korean communities.**[184]

Freedom of speech is something for which Anglos have shed blood. It is a defining value of the English political tradition, along with freedom of association, rule-of-law and representative democracy. It is one of the highest values that has dignified and empowered Anglo society and those who choose to join it.

Free speech allows the powerless to criticise the powerful; it erodes ideological domination. Without freedom of expression, the edifice of civil liberties and reason is compromised. Any group's ability to fight

---

[184] Gawenda, Michael. (2014). The real reason Abbott broke his promise on section 18C. *The Australian*. Sydney, 6 August, https://www.theaustralian.com.au/business/business-spectator/news-story/the-real-reason-abbott-broke-his-promise-on-section-18c/bc977f7be04dc1dab8eb1db52a5707ed, accessed 10.8.2021.

"People have a right to be bigots, says Brandis", *The Australian*, 25 March 2014, p. 5.

"Race act set for radical reshaping", *The Australian*, 18 March 2014, p. 6.

back against oppression and establishment lies, depends on such liberty.

Section 18c of the Racial Discrimination Act 1975 is considered necessary by those who judge Anglos as so dangerous for non-Anglos, so inherently racist, that they need to be punished for speaking words that merely offend. This at a time when traditional taboos – blasphemy, pornography, homosexuality – have been decriminalised despite some people continuing to be offended by them. Anglophobic multiculturalism has changed nothing – except who is in charge.

The joys of diversity are thought to be so fragile that the whole experiment in radical social engineering – mainly the abandonment of assimilationist immigration policy – is deemed at risk of collapsing into mass conflict and white-supremacist tyranny unless the majority have their freedoms curtailed. A tyranny to end all tyranny, it is implied.

This was an assumption motivating the coalition of minority leaders that opposed the Abbott government's attempt to reform Section 18c. Recently arrived immigrants demanded the reduction of a core value of the Australian nation in order to defend their ethnic interests. At the same time, these ethnic enthusiasts insisted that the nation consists of nothing other than values, that Australia has no ethnic core. They propose that values are the only things that define Australia's identity and hold it together; except freedom of speech, an outmoded Anglo-Celtic value not to be tolerated. But the new national values do include *diversity*, which just happens to consist only of non-Anglo identities.

Unsurprisingly they also demand that diversity be tolerated and celebrated.

Antagonism towards Anglo ethnic identity was an integral component of the pro-18c cause. Associated controversies revealed an extraordinary demographic divide. In the prosecution of Andrew Bolt and the attempt to reform Section 18c, one side consisted of leftist lawyers and their minority clients, both with explicit ethnic goals. The other side consisted, by and large, of Anglo conservatives, not explicit in their ethnicity, attempting to defend a precious political tradition from illiberal attack. Free speech has been the first victim of multiculturalism. This pattern has played out repeatedly since the 1970s. On numerous occasions, explicit minority and radical ethnic strategies have defeated implicit Anglo opposition. Adding salt to this particular wound is the fact that it is the Anglos who are accused of racism.

E-2. Should have their expressions of ethnic or cultural pride, solidarity, and identity blocked or removed from media platforms.

The exclusion of individuals who openly and proudly identify as Anglos or who advocate on behalf of them has been a striking feature of the mainstream media since the cultural revolution of the 1960s. Such individuals are denied balanced news reporting, often being criticised or misrepresented. They are prevented from offering commentary. This profound media bias is described by Canadian sociologist Eric Kaufmann in his 2018 book *Whiteshift*, discussed earlier.[185]

In Australia, Anglo pride in identity or concern about interests are rarely reported without censorship or editorial criticism. Anglo advocates are never asked to participate as commentators. This is also true of so-called conservative newspapers and broadcasters. An example is the ethnic bias of *The Australian* newspaper, part of Rupert Murdoch's vast stable of print and broadcast media. This newspaper is considered one of the most right-wing newspapers in the country, despite carrying no reporting or commentary favourable to white identity. However, the newspaper frequently prints stories favourable to Aboriginal and other minority identities or critical of

[185] Kaufmann, E. (2018). *Whiteshift: Populism, immigration, and the future of white majorities*, Penguin.

Salter, F. K. (2019). The ethnic predicaments of the shrinking white majority [part 1]. *Quadrant*. 24 September,

Salter, F. K. (2019). The ethnic predicaments of the shrinking white majority [part 2]. SydneyTrads.com. 2 December,

white identity.[186] The progressive media's bias is more extreme. The effect is to distort news and commentary and create a pervasive media environment that is unfriendly towards Australians who identify as Anglos.

The mainstream media has been biased against Anglo identity for decades, as illustrated by a controversy that emerged in 1984. It involved Professor Geoffrey Blainey, Australia's best-known historian. Blainey received considerable media exposure after he gave a speech in Warrnambool, Victoria, warning that the pace of Asian immigration was outrunning public acceptance. Later that year he published a short book, *All for Australia*, to explain his concerns.[187] The multicultural establishment condemned Blainey for inciting white racism and he was harassed at his university in Melbourne. But he was not and is not on the right. He never publicly affiliated with Anglo identity. He never criticised non-white immigration as a threat to Australia's national identity or to western civilisation on this continent. The professor was concerned about the loss of social cohesion and the rise of domestic conflict.

---

[186] For example, Trinca, H. (2021). 'Racism, tokenism and sexism' in our workplaces. *The Weekend Australian*. Sydney, Newscorp, 26 June, p. 40, https://www.theaustralian.com.au/business/the-deal-magazine/racism-tokenism-and-sexism-in-australian-workplaces/news-story/5970778659318427d62272fa26f9f4e7, accessed 30.6.2021.

[187] Blainey, G. (1984). *All for Australia*. North Ryde, Australia, Methuen Haynes.

Today, traditional print media are in decline and people spend far more time on social media. Social media companies generally allow non-whites to publicly identify with their peoples. This can include language which is divisive, supremacist, derogatory and even threatening. In contrast, even the mildest expression of ethnic identity by Anglos or whites is generally considered to be unacceptable. Alternative social media platforms which have not conformed to this Anglophobic view have been removed from their servers by large tech companies. An example was when the tech giant Amazon removed social media company Parler from its servers in January 2021.[188] Social media platforms are important forums for discussing ideas and sharing information. Locking out anyone who identifies with or advocates for Anglos is itself an act of Anglophobia.

---

[188] Keach Hagey (2021). Parler sues Amazon after Tech giant kicks site off, 11 Jan. 2021. https://www.wsj.com/articles/parler-sues-amazon-kicks-site-off-its-servers-11610363052, accessed 5.8.2021.

F. Must not be allowed a homeland in which they may remain the majority.

Non-white nations of the world are not being pressured to open their borders to allow unlimited immigration of diverse ethnicities. Much of the immigration around the world goes from Third World to developed, mainly white, countries. Anglosphere nations are among the greatest recipients. It is uncontroversial that Japanese people have a right to live in Japan and maintain themselves as a super-majority in their own homeland, as do most other nations.

In white nations, especially in Anglo nations, however, there are well organised and well-funded pressure groups that attack anyone who advocates limiting immigration to protect national identity and prevent diversity reaching dangerous levels. These pressure groups do not specify a cut off point for this immigration. The topic itself is considered off-limits. This suggests that the end point, if not the intention, of these policies is the reduction of Anglo or white majorities until they become minorities in their own countries. That would inevitably result in permanent loss of their power to control policy, including immigration.

The link between political power and the number of voters is real in liberal democracies. Worse, as can be seen from the rest of this document, Anglos' loss of power is accompanied by ever greater Anglophobia. Anglos face the prospect of becoming hated and powerless minorities in the countries they established. Calling for Australia or other Anglophone countries to open their borders to large scale Third World immigration and refugee intakes without advocating the same for all countries is implicitly Anglophobic.

Australia was placed on the path to severing the state from the nation in the 1960s and 1970s when hostile cultural elites came to power. Political scientist David Brown describes how the Australian state was reshaped between 1965 and 1975 to cease supporting the interests of the majority and instead support the interests of minorities.[189] The traditional immigration policy, which protected Anglo-white demographic dominance, was scrapped and replaced by a policy that did not select on ethnic criteria. Expressions of Anglo identity (and only Anglo identity) were suppressed by the media and educational system and by a dedicated UN-specified set of institutions under the Racial Discrimination Act 1975.

Dispossessing a nation of its protective state is a hostile act. In Australia's case it was a form of Anglophobia committed by leaders who avoided democratic process.[190] National identity was never ceded by popular vote.

Malcolm Fraser, Australia's prime minister from 1975 to 1983, was a zealous advocate of multiculturalism. He was also an Anglophobe, declaring: "Anglo-Saxon Australia is dead. This isn't the kind of society we

---

[189] Brown, D. (2000). *Contemporary nationalism. Civic, ethnocultural and multicultural politics*. London, Routledge, pp. 139-140.

[190] Lopez, M. (2000). *The origins of multiculturalism in Australian politics 1945-1975*. Melbourne, Melbourne University Press.

are."[191] He cautioned against allowing Australians a democratic vote on immigration policy, though he advocated broadening the franchise in Rhodesia (now Zimbabwe) and South Africa as a means of ending white rule. In Australia Fraser preferred formulating policies through bipartisan agreement between the major parties, a procedure that helped circumvent democratic consent.[192] By contrast, the Australian Commonwealth was created with broad public support, explicitly to serve the interests of the historic Anglo nation.

The hijacking of the state – in Australia's case the Commonwealth – by hostile elites happened throughout the Anglosphere, resulting in the set of policies that constitute multiculturalism. Kaufmann notes that in the United States, multiculturalism (as practised, not the more principled normative form sold to the public) was from the beginning "asymmetrical", meaning that it excluded and was antagonistic towards Anglo identity and interests.[193]

A clear example of asymmetrical Anglophobic multiculturalism came from Joseph Biden, when he was vice president of the United States during the Obama presidency. In 2015 he declared that it was a

---

[191] Quoted in Lopez, *The origins of multiculturalism in Australian politics 1945-1975.*, p. 440.
[192] Fraser, M. (2003). Common ground: Issues that should bind and not divide us. Camberwell, Victoria, Penguin, pp. 250-251.
[193] Kaufmann, E. (2004). *The rise and fall of Anglo-America.* Cambridge, MA, Harvard University Press, p. 193

good thing that whites would soon become a minority in the United States.

> [The wave of immigration from around the world] it's not gonna stop. Nor should we want it to stop. As a matter of fact … it is one of the things I think we can be most proud of. … [A]n unrelenting stream of immigration, non-stop, non-stop. Folks like me who were Caucasian, of European descent, for the first time in 2017 will be in an absolute minority in the United States of America, absolute minority … That's not a bad thing. That's a, that's a source of our strength.[194]

U.S. statisticians in fact predict that whites will become a minority in the 2040s, though around 2015 they became a minority of children. This factual error does not change the thrust of Biden's wish that America's founding ethnicity lose its majority status; nor does it diminish the prejudice of his view that falling white numbers will somehow strengthen the country. He also pretended that immigration is a force of nature, like the tides, instead of a deliberate choice through public policy and therefore the responsibility of political leaders such as himself. This was an example of the radical pro-diversity ideology adopted

---

[194] Biden, J. (2015). Remarks by the Vice President at a State Department luncheon for the Brazilian President, 30 June. https://www.youtube.com/watch?v=peF-ae2AINU, accessed 6.11.2020.

The official State Department record of the event offers only an abridged version of Biden's words. "Remarks at a Luncheon in Honor of President of Brazil Dilma Rousseff" 30 June 2015, https://2009-2017.state.gov/s/d/2015/244515.htm, accessed 25.2.2022.

by Anglophobic elites. It is an insurrection against the nation. Similarly, Australia's immigration policy is what one would expect from those who are indifferent or actually hostile to Anglo-Australia's interests.

It should be noted that normative multiculturalism, though superior to the racist Anglophobic type found in Australia, is far from perfect. Its democratic, egalitarian aspects are attractive – that is why they are proclaimed.

Like its ruthless Anglophobic doppelganger, however, it bears the marks of utopian doctrine. For example, it ignores the costs of ethno-religious diversity. Ethnic conflict and inequality are caused by the interaction of different ethnicities; they are not caused by Anglos or whites or Christians alone.

All ethnicities have interests that can conflict in diverse societies. Group differences in talents and interests contribute to ethnic class stratification which further embitters relations. Normative multiculturalism ignores or denies these facts because it is an ideology developed to advance minority interests; it is not a disinterested pursuit of truth. The doctrine is more noble than its real-world racist twin, but historically has always been window dressing for it.

It is hostile discrimination to excoriate whites for small discriminations or merely for expressing pride in identity while at the same time normalising and praising the more intense solidarity that is common among minorities. This double standard is at the heart of both normative and Anglophobic multiculturalism. The enforcement of "rules for thee, not for me" reveals an ethnic hierarchy which was forming by the 1960s.

Anglophobic multiculturalists openly commit this double standard. An example is American demographer Joel Kotkin who valorises minority networking in business. This entails systematic solidarity of the "tribe" and exclusion of outsiders. At the same time, he condemns white solidarity, which he calls "white nationalism" and "racism".[195]

Multiculturalism in Australia and other Anglosphere nations has followed a similar pattern. Professor Andrew Fraser (no relation to Malcolm Fraser), concluded in his 2011 book *The Wasp Question* that by the 1970s Anglos around the world had become a stateless people. The states they created – in Australia, Canada, the United States, New Zealand and in their country of origin, Britain – had been turned against them.[196]

Bob Carr provides us with one such example of political elites opposing Anglo identity and interests. Carr was once premier of New South Wales and later

---

[195] Kotkin, Joel. (1992). *Tribes: How race, religion and identity determine success in the new global economy*. New York, Random House.

Kotkin, Joel. Elites: The new ruling class? Interviewed by John Anderson, 2 July 2021.
https://www.youtube.com/watch?v=SDO1zhDi7Bl, accessed 23.7.2021.

[196] Fraser, Andrew. (2011). *The WASP question: An essay on the biocultural evolution, present predicament, and future prospects of the invisible race*. London, Arktos.

See also:

Fraser, Andrew. (2005/2006). The White Australia Policy in retrospect: Racism or realism? *The Occidental Quarterly* 5(4): 7-29.

became foreign minister of Australia under prime minister Julia Gillard. He adopted informed positions on a range of issues, but was also a doctrinaire multiculturalist of the reflexive, Anglophobic kind. This emerged clearly in remarks he made shortly after the death of Baroness Margaret Thatcher in 2013. Because Carr was Australia's foreign minister at the time, his critical comments were reported internationally. Carr accused Thatcher of making "unabashedly racist" comments to him in private after her retirement. She had warned Australia against large-scale Asian immigration. He recalled Thatcher saying words to the effect that "if we allowed too much [Asian immigration] we'd see the natives of the land, the European settlers, overtaken by migrants.". He also reported Thatcher saying: "You will end up like Fiji. … I like Sydney, but you can't allow the migrants to take over, otherwise you will end up like Fiji where the Indian migrants have taken over."

Carr claimed to have been "astonished" at the comments by Lady Thatcher, the more so as they were made while his Malaysian-born wife was standing nearby but "fortunately out of earshot". "I couldn't believe it." He judged Thatcher to have been "old-fashioned" and "entirely out of touch".[197]

The aspiration to remain the majority ethnicity in one's own country is completely normal, ethical and, for non-white nations, uncontroversial. Thatcher's

---

[197] Carr, B. (2013). BBC News (2013). Margaret Thatcher 'racist' – Australian minister Bob Carr, 9 April, http://www.bbc.co.uk/news/world-asia-22087702, accessed 16.12.2021.

remarks were not racist, they were ethnocentric. She did not express dislike for Asians. She simply expressed affection and concern for white Australians. She acknowledged different identities and implied that becoming a minority would not be in the interests of the Anglo Australians whose forebears had built the nation. Moreover, she expressed sympathy for the Fijians who felt the same way. Thatcher's remarks about Fiji indicate that she was speaking from principle, not only special affection for Australia. Thatcher opined that Indians had overtaken the native Fijians, a view widely shared in Fiji and the source of much upheaval as Fijians sought to retain control of their country.

Especially puzzling is Carr's defensive attitude about his wife. Was he implying that it is reasonable for an Asian immigrant to object to Australia's historical identity? For most of Australia's history we have been a nation descended from European settlers.

If Carr had emigrated to Malaysia, would it have been reasonable for him to take offence to hear ethnic Malays described as natives of the country? Has he objected to ethnic Malays calling themselves the "Bumiputra", meaning "son of the soil"? If Malaysia had been receiving white immigrants in numbers that threatened to swamp the local population or wrest political or economic control from them, on what grounds would a white immigrant be offended by Malays expressing concern? A genuine social democrat or anyone of empathy and humanitarian impulse, would surely sympathise.

G. May have their cultural and religious traditions trivialised, denigrated or eradicated.

Currently in western nations the policy of multiculturalism encourages different ethnic groups to retain, celebrate, pass on and feel pride in their ethnic, cultural, and religious heritages.[198] The only people discouraged from doing so are those of European descent in general (whites), and Anglos in particular.

Long ago explicit Anglo identity became marginalised in public enactments and memorials. School curricula denigrated Anglo history. Their statues, monuments and place names are threatened with defacement or removal.[199]

Anglo-Australia's public commemorations are also criticised. The most important is Anzac Day, when veterans march in towns and cities throughout the nation to remember the fallen. Professor Eva Cox at the University of Technology, Sydney, doubted that Anzac Day was for all Australians because it is "very Anzac Anglo".[200] The allegedly conservative Aboriginal activist Noel Pearson considers Anzac Day too

---

[198] *Community Relations Commission and Principles of Multiculturalism Act 2000* No 77. https://legislation.nsw.gov.au/inforce/a6ac573d-70ec-61e7-c63e-9e43748c3306/2000-77.pdf, accessed 10 Sept. 2019.

[199] Furedi, F. (2021). Rioters are blurring lines between present and past. *Weekend Australian*. Sydney, News Corporation, 13 Feb., p. 14. https://www.theaustralian.com.au/inquirer/rioters-are-blurring-lines-between-present-and-past/news-story/00dfb3f5d2af51ad82db515f0a8e1ede, accessed 4.5.2021.

[200] Eva Cox, in *The Sun Herald*, 29 April 2012, p. 86.

white and finds it nauseating that whites do not instead remember his own people's suffering.[201]

Another day of commemoration is Australia Day, which celebrates the arrival of the First Fleet from Britain in 1788. Peter Gebhardt, a retired County Court Judge, wrote: "Australia Day is, of course, an artificial fabrication designed by governments . . . and smug Anglo-Saxons to ensure that we forget real history. That Anglo-Saxon smugness is a resilient child of hypocrisy and racism".[202]

Perhaps the oldest form of Anglophobia has been Christophobia, the hatred of the traditional religion of the British Isles since the seventh century AD and of large areas of Europe before then. Despite being a universalist religion, Christianity is historically bound to Europe and the civilisation it created. The New Testament was originally written in Greek and became the state religion of the Roman Empire, spreading to the rest of Europe and beyond during the Empire and following its collapse. Before the emergence of national consciousness, the largest identity groups were religiously defined. During the Middle Ages, from before the Muslim invasions, Europe was known as "Christendom". The first description of the emerging English nation was by the Benedictine monk, the Venerable Bede, in about 731 AD. European global

---

[201] Noel Pearson, 2011, *Up from the mission: Selected writings*, Collingwood, Victoria: Schwartz Media, p. 337.

[202] Peter Gebhardt, "Nation's day a chance to shine a light into the darkness", *The Sydney Morning Herald,* 26 Jan. 2012.

exploration and colonisation bore the cross as well as the sextant, musket, and trade goods.

The days of expansive Christian power, however, are long gone. Like western demographics, Christianity has been in retreat for many decades. Persecution of Christians is prevalent in many parts of the world today, particularly in Islamic countries where discrimination is routine and violence common. World surveys show that Christians are, in fact, more persecuted than members of any other religions. For example, a Pew study found that between 2006 and 2010 Christians were subjected to harassment, mainly from governments, in 139 countries, more than any other religion.[203]

Christianity has been in decline in the West for more than a century, but hostility towards the religion has accelerated in the last few decades, a period which coincides with mass immigration from non-western and non-Christian countries. At the same time there has been a push by elites to remove Christianity and its symbols from everyday life. Examples of denigration of and hostility towards Christianity are too numerous to mention but some notable examples follow.

As previously mentioned, an example of racist Christophobia in popular culture is the book, *The Chant of Jimmy Blacksmith* by Thomas Keneally (1972), and its film adaptation by Fred Schepisi

---

[203] Grim, B. J. et al. (2014). Rising tide of restrictions on religion, *The Pew Forum on Religion & Public Life*, Pew Research Center, September 2012, https://www.pewforum.org/2012/09/20/rising-tide-of-restrictions-on-religion-findings/, p. 23, accessed 12.10.2021.

(1978). In the film version especially, Methodist missionaries are mocked and pathologized. This, combined with the Anglo identity of the victims, gives a distinctly racial overtone to the book's Christophobia. One reviewer, Mark Fraser, notes that the film oversimplifies the racial dimension and fabricates the Church's role. "[B]oth as a book and a movie, [it] involves a couple of white guys (Schepisi and Keneally) using the story of a victimised Aborigine as an excuse to attack one of their bugbears – Christians."[204]

The terms "BC" and "AD" have been at the cornerstone of the western calendar for millennia. They stand for "Before Christ" and "Anno Domini" (Year of our Lord). In many western countries these terms are being challenged by Christophobes, without popular support. Attempts are being made to replace the terms with "CE" and "BCE", which stand for "Common Era" and "Before the Common Era".[205]

The festival of Christmas, practised for centuries across the West, is under attack, though not as severely in Australia as in Britain and the United States. Gift cards now bear terms such as "Happy Holidays" or

---

[204] Fraser, M. (2020). Review: "The Chant of Jimmie Blacksmith" is no church hymn, *Top 10 Films*, 9 January, https://www.top10films.co.uk/56966-review-the-chant-of-jimmie-blacksmith-is-no-church-hymn/, accessed 25.10.2021.

[205] In Britain militant secularists have been replacing the use of "BC" and "AD" in schools since 2012 at the latest. E.g. Das-Gupta, I. (2012). AD and BC become CE/BCE. *The Evening Standard (London),* 12 April, https://www.standard.co.uk/hp/front/ad-and-bc-become-ce-bce-6330342.html, accessed 12.10.2021.

"Winter Wishes" instead of the traditional "Happy Christmas". The British Red Cross has removed nativity scenes from its shops for fear of retribution against its charity workers.[206] Peter Brimelow, once editor of *Forbes* Magazine, first identified a "war on Christmas" in 1999 and has provided examples of the war being part of a larger assault on white America.[207]

Christophobia is more extreme outside western countries. Asia Bibi was a Christian farm worker from Pakistan who in 2009 was accused of blasphemy and sentenced to death after a disagreement with other farm workers who did not want a Christian drinking from the same well as Muslims. After eight years on death row, Bibi was acquitted on appeal but continued to be threatened by lynch mobs. She applied for asylum in several western nations but her claims were rejected by the UK government who were afraid of a violent backlash from newly arrived Islamic citizens.[208]

---

[206] AFP (2002). British Red Cross bans Christmas: Report. *The Sydney Morning Herald*. Sydney, Fairfax, 22 December, https://www.smh.com.au/world/british-red-cross-bans-christmas-report-20021222-gdg07m.html, accessed 12.10.2021.

[207] Fulford, J. (2010). "The war against Christmas 2010: God bless us, every one! https://vdare.com/articles/the-war-against-christmas-2010-god-bless-us-every-one, 24 December, accessed 12.10.2021."

[208] Farmer, B. (2018). Asia Bibi 'not offered UK asylum amid concerns of unrest and attacks'. *The Telegraph* (London), 11 November, https://www.telegraph.co.uk/news/2018/11/11/asia-bibi-not-offered-uk-asylum-amid-concerns-unrest-attacks/, accessed 12.10.2021.
https://www.huffingtonpost.co.uk/entry/britain-not-prepared-to-offer-asylum-to-persecuted-pakistani-

In India in 1999 Graham Staines, a 55 year old Australian Christian missionary, was **burnt to death** along with his two sons, aged 8 and 10, by a mob of more than 100 Hindu extremists. Mr Staines had been working with leprosy patients in India for more than 30 years. The attack came at the end of two years of Hindu extremist attacks on Christians and churches.[209]

While Christian belief and heritage are not unique to Anglos, they are historically identified with them and other western peoples, especially in the minds of many non-Anglos. This is revealed by "intersectionality", one idea of Critical Race Theory that makes sense. Intersectionality theory was developed in the late 1980s at Chicago University.[210] It occurs where an individual has multiple identities each of which attracts disadvantage. Typical examples raised by the left are black women and black men. Both can be discriminated against for their race, which is compounded, in the example of black women, by discrimination against their sex. A popular example

christian_uk_5be3342be4b0dbe871a61b95, accessed 12.10.2021.

[209] CSW (1999). Australian missionary and two sons burnt to death by Hindu extremists in India, https://www.csw.org.uk/1999/01/25/press/129/article.htm, accessed 12.10.2021.

http://news.bbc.co.uk/1/hi/world/south_asia/261391.stm, accessed 12.10.2021.

[210] Crenshaw, K. (1989). "Demarginalizing the intersection of race and sex: A black feminist critique of antidiscrimination doctrine, feminist theory and antiracist politics." *University of Chicago Legal Forum* 1989(1): 139-167, https://chicagounbound.uchicago.edu/cgi/viewcontent.cgi?article=1052&context=uclf, accessed 5.5.2021.

among conservatives is straight white Christian males. Suffering from this four-way intersectionality is exacerbated because the constituent discriminations are often enforced or advocated by governments, schools, and corporations. This legal discrimination takes the form of group defamation and affirmative action, formal and informal. The most extreme Anglophobic vilification is reserved for heterosexual white Christian men.

8. Examining Types of Anglophobia: *Hostile Discrimination*

The foregoing examples of vilification could not occur if cultural elites were not motivated by animus towards Anglo-Australia. This has been apparent for many decades. The same animus motivates hostile discrimination. In 1994 the great Australian poet, the late Les Murray, complained that the cultural elites ...

> are discriminatory, they exclude. 'They' are not just the Australia Council; they are the ruling elite of today's Australia: the cultural bureaucrats, the academics, the intellectuals ... They are excluding people like me from their Australia – the country people, the rednecks, the Anglo-Celts, the farming people – they have turned their backs on us. They act as though they despise us . . . We Old Australians, not always Anglo but having no other country but this one, are now mostly caught and silenced between the indigenous and the multicultural.[211]

Murray was reacting against the racial politics of the time. When he wrote, the Hawke-Keating Labor governments were still in power. The Labor Party was using multiculturalism in the form of identity politics

---

[211] Quoted in Paul Sheehan (1998). *Among the barbarians*, p. 141.

to increase its votes among the non-Anglo, largely immigrant, population. The initial foray into Anglophobic multiculturalism by the Fraser Liberal government (1975-1983) had already been ramped up. In the Labor Party, ethnic branch stacking was practised on a large scale, with favours dispensed by government in exchange for votes and immigration favours.[212] *Sydney Morning Herald* journalist Paul Sheehan noted at the time that the Hawke and Keating governments assiduously cultivated the non-English speaking migrant vote in Sydney and Melbourne. More than a billion dollars of taxpayer money was spent on "building a system of patronage, dependence and influence among ethnic groups".[213] Political multiculturalism from its earliest days involved systematic ethnic discrimination – the exclusion and over-taxation of Anglo-Australians.

As previously noted, Anglo Australians are routinely discriminated against in employment and promotion, despite (or perhaps because of) an elaborate system of "equal employment opportunity" (EEO) legislation and accompanying bureaucracies. The EEO and Affirmative Action (AA) regimes are designed and managed to benefit designated victim groups, which exclude Anglos as a category. As a result, ethnic affirmative action amounts to jobs and promotions being taken from Anglos and given to others.

---

[212] Healy, E. (1993). "Ethnic ALP branches – the Balkanisation of Labor." *People and Place* 1(4): 37-43.

Allan, L. (2002). "ALP modernisation, ethnic branch stacking, factionalism and the law." *People and Place* 10(4): 50-58.

[213] Sheehan, *Among the Barbarians*, p. 99.

The EEO and AA apparatus installed in government and corporate bureaucracies has doctrinal and organisational links to the multicultural establishment. With rare exceptions its officers are not concerned about protecting the rights of Anglo-Australians as an ethnic category. This misdirection of priorities can be harmful. An example was the death of hundreds of elderly, mainly Anglo, Australians during the Covid 19 pandemic in Melbourne in 2020, due to the incompetence of a security firm hired by the Victorian government to manage hotel isolation. It appears the company hired to provide security for much of the hotel quarantine program was chosen because it was majority Aboriginal-owned. The government's affirmative action program for indigenous firms was labelled a "social inclusion procurement policy".[214] Between March and July 2020 the company received a much greater dollar value of contracts than two rival companies listed on the government's panel of pre-approved security suppliers despite the company not being listed on the panel.[215] As a result of security failures at the quarantine hotels, Covid 19 infections killed over 700 Australians in 2020.

A major category of Anglophobic discrimination is the censorship of Anglo advocates from the mainstream media and the new social media, discussed in point 5a

---

[214] Banned security boss David Millward 'never left', *The Australian*, 14.4.2021.
https://www.theaustralian.com.au/nation/politics/banned-security-boss-david-millward-never-left/news-story/80d1faed7824a1617669591a1473e679, accessed 7.7.2021.

[215] Unified Security boss says not its fault virus escaped hotel quarantine, *The Age*, 6.11.2020. accessed 7.7.2021.

above. Anglos who express pride in their identity or who advocate for their people have been routinely barred from the corporate media since the Second World War, especially from the 1960s onwards. They are also "cancelled" from the new web-based social media such as Twitter (pre-Musk), Facebook, and You Tube, while other identity groups are not. Multicultural advocates are left undisturbed in such institutions.

Exclusion of Anglos from public institutions has returned many western societies to the days of racial segregation. The new social media even resort to an old argument used by white segregationists right up to the 1960s. They claim that private businesses have a right to choose to whom they provide services. That was the rationale behind hotels and shops putting out signs banning blacks. The US supreme court overturned this right in the 1960s. Now Twitter, Facebook, You Tube, Amazon and ancillary services such as PayPal routinely cancel white conservatives and white advocates on the grounds that they, as private companies, can discriminate as they like. The result is a privatised version of Jim Crow, the system used in Southern states after the Civil War to prevent African Americans from voting. Being prevented from using social media is arguably more isolating and marginalising than being prevented from voting.

The resemblance to segregation is being heightened by comparison with small social media sites such as Gab, Bitchute, Odysee and others which, because of their freer-speech standards, present a diversity that includes Anglo and white advocates. But due to the large market share of mainstream social media, their Anglophobia has nevertheless created a society-wide hostile environment in which whites are subjected to isolation, systemic racism and stigmatisation.

There are signs that similar censorship is now being extended to Anglos who are not ethnic advocates. An example was provided by Professor Ian Hickie, a psychologist at the University of Sydney, who objected to the number of male Anglo officials managing the government's response to the Covid pandemic. None of these officials were claiming Anglo identity or loyalty. They were performing duties that went with their public offices. Nevertheless, Professor Hickie suggested replacing these faces and their Anglo values with those of other races. The values Prof. Hickie claimed were being forced on the population were "Anglo cultural norms of top-down command and control structures, rule-of-law, and individual accountability". Such values were not given top priority by non-Anglos, Hickie maintained. "Could some press conferences be led by people speaking in languages other than English (with subtitles or translations for those of us who are still monolingual)?" "Could the daily briefings be led by more representative community leaders, with less emphasis on prolonged updates by predominantly Anglo politicians, health officials or men in uniform?"[216] In other words, Anglos can annoy and offend just by being who they are, without any

---

[216] Hickie, I. (2021). Talk about un-Australian: our Anglo, male pandemic commanders do not speak for much of the nation. *The Sydney Morning Herald*. Sydney, Fairfax, 14 August, https://www.smh.com.au/national/talk-about-un-australian-our-anglo-male-pandemic-commanders-do-not-speak-for-much-of-the-nation-20210812-p58ic7.html.

declaration of identity or white advocacy. And, it is suggested, they should be removed from their roles on the basis of their ethnic identity. A clearer example of hostile discrimination is difficult to imagine.

Another form of discrimination consists of ignoring Anglo disadvantage. The ABC and corporate media treat Aboriginal deaths in custody as a major concern.[217] That is Anglophobic because since 2003 non-Aboriginals, of which Anglos are the largest fraction, have suffered higher per capita rates of deaths in custody, but receive no sympathy from the media. Misleading reports of elevated rates of Aboriginal deaths in custody are occasions for politicised content that tends to shame whites and pressure governments. What is shocking is the very high rate of indigenous incarceration, which is several times the per capita white rate. Once in gaol, however, Aboriginals have lower deaths rates than whites.

A 1996 report by the Human Rights Commission provided a different finding for the period 1990 to 1995 – that Aboriginal deaths in custody per 1,000 prisoners were 1.26 times higher than for non-Aborigines.[218] This report is misleading. The royal commission into the subject began work in 1987, reporting in 1991. It compared rates of deaths in custody from 1981 to that

---

[217] For example, the ABC news program *7:30*, broadcast on 15.7.2021.
[218] Australian Human Rights Commission (1996-presumed). *Indigenous deaths in custody*: Chapter 3. https://humanrights.gov.au/our-work/indigenous-deaths-custody-chapter-3-comparison-indigenous-and-non-indigenous-deaths, accessed 15.7.2021.

date. Research has continued, providing comparisons until at least 2016.[219] From 1981 to 2003 the Aboriginal and non-Aboriginal rates spent roughly an equal time in excess. From 2003 the non-indigenous rate overtook the indigenous rate, though the difference has not been great.

Whatever the excuse or rationale, discrimination against Anglo-Australians tends to acquire Anglophobic connotations. An example from the 1990s was recounted by *Sydney Morning Herald* columnist Paul Sheehan. It concerned a leaked memo from a manager at SBS, a television channel sponsored by the government to provide content for ethnic minorities. The memo commented on an application for a managerial position at the broadcaster. "We don't need someone from that sort of background, an Anglo. An Anglo shouldn't be given that job; it should go to an ethnic. … How can she know what the ethnic community needs? She's an Australian."[220] Had the situation been reversed, it would have been considered intolerable, and heads, jobs and reputations would have rolled.

A severe form of discrimination against Anglos is the use of the educational system to indoctrinate school children. An example of institutional Anglophobia in

---

[219] Deaths in prison custody 1981 to 2016; rate per 100 prisoners.
https://www.creativespirits.info/aboriginalculture/law/royal-commission-into-aboriginal-deaths-in-custody, accessed 15.7.2021.

[220] Sheehan, P. (1998). *Among the barbarians: The dividing of Australia.* Sydney, Random House Australia, p. 139.

Australia's educational system is the *Melbourne Declaration on Educational Goals for Young Australians*, published in 2008.[221] Since the 1960s, Australian and other western educational systems had been suffering from the colonisation of the university sector by intolerant left ideology. The *Declaration* was one step in that process. It has been used to set the National Curriculum, as explained by ACARA, the Australian Curriculum, Assessment and Reporting Authority. ACARA states that the *Melbourne Declaration* is its guide to education policy, practice and delivery in Australian schools.[222]

The *Melbourne Declaration* is a radical document because it states that school curricula should emphasise the study of indigenous culture, Asia, and environmentalism. It does not mention Australia's heritage of British or European culture, though in 2008 Anglo-Australians were still the country's majority identity. Nor does it mention Australia being part of

---

[221] Dawkins, P., M. Banks, M. Bruniges, M. Coutts-Trotter, B. Croke, R. Dullard, B. Daniel, L. Foster, R. Hunter, B. McGaw, T. Mackay, S. O'Neill, L. Paul, C. Robinson, J. Smyth, B. Burmester, N. Jeffrey and L. Loble (2008). *Melbourne declaration on educational goals for young Australians*, Ministerial Council on Education, Employment, Training and Youth Affairs, http://www.curriculum.edu.au/verve/_resources/national_declaration_on_the_educational_goals_for_young_australians.pdf, accessed 6 July 2021.

[222] ACARA (The Australian Curriculum, Assessment and Reporting Authority), https://www.acara.edu.au/reporting/national-report-on-schooling-in-australia/nrosia2009/national-policy-context/educational-goals, accessed 5 July 2021.

western civilisation. "Anglo" and "British" are not in the *Declaration*. Nor is "heritage" or "origins" or "western" or "canon" or "Greek" or "Roman" or "Christian" or "European" or "Europe". Nor "pioneers", "identity", or "Shakespeare". The same omissions apply to documents derived from the *Declaration*, such as the National Curriculum.[223]

The *Declaration*'s first goal includes promoting equity,[224] also a goal of affirmative action. A definition of equitable opportunity is offered that gives indigenous students and communities greater emphasis than all other ethnicities combined – "ensur[ing] that schools build on local cultural knowledge and experience of Indigenous students as a foundation for learning, and work in partnership with local communities on all aspects of the schooling process, including to promote high expectations for the learning outcomes of Indigenous students". The definition is then expanded to include *outcomes* – "ensur[ing] that the learning outcomes of Indigenous students improve to match those of other students". In left-liberal ideology, "equity" means equal outcomes. It is not limited to equal opportunities, because equalising opportunity allows for unequal outcomes among individuals and groups all of whom are decreed to be equal in talents and interests. In reality there are differences, sometimes significant ones, between individuals and groups. The result is that a choice must

---

[223] The Australian Curriculum (2021).
   https://www.australiancurriculum.edu.au/, accessed 16.9.2021.
[224] The Australian Curriculum, p. 7.

be made between equality of opportunity and equality of outcomes. By insisting on equal outcomes, the state must discriminate against non-favoured groups such as Anglos in the attempt to produce the desired equality.

These goals omit naming any identity other than indigeneity. If the system was fair and equitable, Anglo communities, the majority and core of national identity, would be especially drawn upon to provide culture and experience. Under-performing individuals of any background, including white males, would be encouraged to improve. The emphasis on Aboriginal education is discriminatory in a way that is most harmful to Anglo Australia.

Another stated goal of the *Declaration* is to "ensure that schooling contributes to a socially cohesive society that respects and appreciates cultural, social and religious diversity". As mentioned previously, "diversity" is often used as a leftist dog whistle meaning "less white". Therefore, doctrinaire emphasis on diversity is bound to reduce the teaching of Australia's historic Anglo and western civilisation. In fact, the *Declaration's* diversity agenda pushes aside the Anglo and western canons altogether. It is a reasonable expectation that Australian students of all backgrounds should learn who Australia's founders, developers and population were for most of the nation's history. These people were largely Anglos, including people who had assimilated into that culture. Students should know that the Australian nation was a product of western peoples and civilisation.

The *Declaration* is an Anglophobic document that would erase Australia's history and distort its culture.

Though it relegates all non-indigenous peoples, it demotes Anglo-Australians the most by implying that the historic Anglo nation is just another contending ethnicity, identified only as "non-indigenous".

The *Melbourne Declaration* cannot be blamed on any particular side of politics. It is a manifestation of a broader culture war. When it was officially adopted, the Labor Party controlled the federal and most state governments. However, so-called conservative governments have not rescinded official endorsement of the document nor abolished its enabling legislation and bureaucracies. They have not even criticised the *Declaration* or appointed inquiries into how such a monumental act of governmental racism could have been produced by universities and the senior public service or accepted by the mainstream media.

Of course, it would have been inconsistent for "conservatives" to oppose this document whilst enthusiastically supporting multiculturalism and the mass replacement immigration it legitimates. The same complicity applies to the promotion of Aboriginal nationalism in schools – the mandatory flying of the Aboriginal flag with equal prominence to the national flag and the enforcement of the "Acknowledgment of Country" ritual at school assemblies, both of which lend credibility to indigenous claims to national territory ahead of the foundational claim by the historic Anglo nation. The institutional racism, of which the *Melbourne Declaration* and Acknowledgment of Country ritual are parts, has flourished due to the bipartisan acceptance of Anglophobic discrimination by mainstream political parties.

Conservative irresolution and confusion in the face of academic Anglophobia goes back many years. It is a symptom of the triumphant march of the intolerant left through the universities. According to analysts such as Eric Kaufmann, left liberals dominated the humanities and social sciences in the US by the 1950s. This was documented in his ground-breaking book, *The Rise and Fall of Anglo America*, discussed earlier. Australia fits this trend, with Anglophobic ideologues occupying high positions in the university system. The corporate media often give a platform to these radicals. One example is a 2017 documentary shown on SBS Television, *Is Australia Racist?* Hosted by Ray Martin, the program interviewed four academics all with track records of criticising Anglo Australia. Three were senior professors – Andrew Markus, Andrew Jakubowicz, and Kevin Dunn.

Andrew Markus's attacks on Anglo society go back to his doctoral dissertation at La Trobe University in the 1970s when he criticised Australian and American restrictive immigration policy following the gold rushes of the 19th century. Markus is part of the multicultural establishment. For many years he has been the lead researcher of the influential Scanlon Surveys of social attitudes across the nation, which are routinely circulated to members of the Federal Parliament and accepted respectfully by the media. Marcus attributes ethnic conflict to Anglo intolerance and offers blanket defences of multiculturalism and mass immigration.[225]

---

[225] Salter, F. K. (2018). The inherent racism of SBS's multiculturalism, Part II. The academic experts.

Professor Andrew Jakubowicz's anti-white animus was discussed in Section 3C. He has been highly placed in the NSW educational establishment and favoured by corporate media as an adviser, including on Ray Martin's program.

Professor Kevin Dunn is presently the "Pro Vice-Chancellor Research" at Macquarie University. His research has been funded by the academic and multicultural establishments. He uses tropes from Critical Race Theory to study racism and ethnic discrimination but only, it would seem, when these acts are committed by mainstream Australians. He is not interested in the plight of Anglos when they suffer ethnic swamping, discrimination or violence. This includes an odd form of racism. When Anglo-Australians deny that Australia is racist, Dunn takes this as evidence of their racism. Anglo guilt and privilege are treated as axiomatic, as is immigrant victimhood. For example, Dunn states that the "new racism" is a distinctly Anglo view of the nation as assimilationist or egalitarian. He argues that it is racist to assert the equality of all Australians, because, according to him, this denies white privilege.[226]

These professors are the tip of the Anglophobic iceberg in our universities, particularly prominent in the humanities and soft social sciences. Consider one more example, an influential book, *Mistaken identity:*

SydneyTrads.com: June,
https://sydneytrads.com/2018/06/15/inherent-racism-of-multiculturalism-pt1/

[226] Salter, F. K. (2018). The inherent racism of SBS's multiculturalism, Part II.

Multiculturalism and the demise of nationalism in Australia, which was published in 1992.[227] The book argues that Australia as a nation state is both undesirable and impossible. The book's authors call for Australia's national symbols to be continually smashed using mass education to inculcate in children guilt for alleged genocide against Aborigines. "Above all, the history of white racism and genocide against the Aborigines must become a central theme of education and public debate, and an accommodation with the Aborigines must be achieved through payment of reparations and Land Rights legislation." (p. 367)

The book was not produced by impoverished revolutionaries at the fringes of Australia's universities. Consider the lead author, Stephen Castles, whose globalist credentials are impeccable. A sociologist and political economist specialising in international migration and its transformatory effects, he has advised the British and Australian governments and has worked for the International Labour Organisation, the International Organisation for Migration, the European Union and other international organisations. By 2012 he was Research Chair in Sociology at Sydney University. Earlier in his career, at Wollongong University, he was, like Andrew Jakubowicz, director of the Centre for Multicultural Studies (1986-1996) and director of the Centre for Asia Pacific Social Transformation Studies.

---

[227] Castles, S., B. Cope, M. Kalantzis and M. Morrissey (1992). *Mistaken identity: Multiculturalism and the demise of nationalism in Australia.* Sydney, Pluto Press.

The radicals advocating the deconstruction of western societies in general and Anglophone countries in particular are no longer shouting from the streets at the establishment. From the 1980s at the latest they were an influential part of the establishment. Anglophobes are part of the academic mainstream. Theirs is a top-down revolution. It is their patriotic opponents who are marginalised and whose livelihoods and reputations are in peril.

9. Examining Types of Anglophobia: *Violence*

From Federation to the 1970s ethnic violence in Australia, including anti-white violence, was rare. This was because the country had an established, dominant ethnic group and ethno-religious diversity was low. That situation began to change when hostile elites took control of immigration policy, beginning in the early 1970s. For some time, diversity remained low compared to strife-torn regions such as sub-Saharan Africa, the Indian subcontinent, and parts of South East Asia. The trend of rising diversity and ethnic conflict accelerated in the 1990s. Thankfully, Australia's economically selective immigration system has avoided much potential violence. Nevertheless, some immigrant and refugee groups that have settled in Australia have shown relatively high rates of criminality, including violence directed at the native-born Anglo population. Notable examples are the anti-Anglo rape culture of the late 1990s and jihadist terrorism that developed among a minority of the Muslim community.[228]

---

[228] The article that first revealed the ethnic nature of the rapes, both of intent and organisation, was Chulov, M. (2001). Rape menace from the melting pot. *The Weekend Australian.* Sydney, News Corporation, 18-19 August.

In Sydney in 2000 a gang of fourteen young ethnic Lebanese Muslim men – the children of immigrants brought to Australia in the 1970s by prime minister Malcolm Fraser[229] – conducted a series of pack rapes explicitly targeting white, mainly Anglo, girls, aged 14 to 18. More than fifty girls were assaulted, a forerunner of the mass rapes of English girls in Rotherham (described at the end of this section). The ethnic dimension was evident in the fact that all the rapists were Lebanese Muslims and all or most the victims were Anglos. Ethnic motivation was confirmed when one target of the attacks reported that the perpetrators called her an "Aussie pig" and called themselves Lebanese.[230] Another rapist told a victim that she deserved to be raped "because you're Australian".[231]

The article was originally published in the Sydney *Sun-Herald*, 29 July 2001. It is reproduced in:

James, A. (2013). *New Britannia: The rise and decline of Anglo-Australia*. Melbourne, Lulu.com, pp. 171-174.

[229] Anderson, Stephanie. (2016). Peter Dutton suggests Fraser government made mistake by resettling Lebanese refugees, ABC News, 22 November, https://www.abc.net.au/news/2016-11-21/peter-dutton-fraser-made-mistake-resettling-lebanese-refugees/8043624, accessed 16.11.2021.

[230] Bowden, T. (2002). "Ethnicity linked to brutal gang rapes, ABC Television, 15 July, https://web.archive.org/web/20070108091135/http://www.abc.net.au/7.30/content/2002/s607757.htm, accessed 19.9.2021." Retrieved 19 Sept. 2021.

[231] Goodenough, P. (2002). "Gang rape convictions trigger ethnicity debate." *CNSnews.com*, 16 July, https://web.archive.org/web/20060524105853/http://www.cnsnews.com/ViewForeignBureaus.asp?Page=%5CForeignBureaus%5Carchive%5C200207%5CFOR20020716b.html, accessed 15.6.2021.

New South Wales director of public prosecutions asserted a clear ethnic motive for the rapes.[232]

In 2021 the main perpetrators were reported to be eligible for parole. ABC Television reviewed the rapes of 21 years earlier but failed to mention the ethnic dimension or the fact that these were hate crimes.[233] This dimension of the crimes was censored. The mainstream media, including the ABC, appear more concerned with obscuring hate crimes committed against Anglos than informing the public of their full causes. The same outlets are ever ready to report this type of crime when committed against minorities.

Jihadist terrorism became a security concern beginning in 2003. Many attacks have occurred on Australian soil, whilst others have been prevented by the authorities. This, however, was not the only form of organised crime committed by members of immigrant minorities.

Crime by immigrant communities became such a problem that the New South Wales and Victorian state governments established special ethnic crime divisions with the skills and focus to tackle ethnically organised crime. In the 1980s and 1990s Asian Crime Squads were established in NSW and Victoria. In 2006 NSW established the Middle East Organised Crime Squad, following the Cronulla Riots (see below). The Squad was based on an earlier body, Task Force Gain, set up in 2003 in response to shootings in South West

---

[232] Goodenough, "Gang rape convictions trigger ethnicity debate".
[233] ABC Television News, 17.9.2021.

Sydney. Some of this criminality was ethnically directed. Police in South-West Sydney were aware of widespread harassment and violence against whites, mainly by youths from the Islamic community.[234] Ethnic crime squads were disbanded by 2017 not because the crime wave had receded but due to the claim that gangs had become less ethnically bounded.[235]

Though some of the violence directed against Anglos was not ethnically motivated, by 2008 white and Asian students were being driven out of public schools in areas of Sydney and Melbourne. A survey conducted by the University of Western Sydney in 2008 found that one in four male students surveyed in Sydney's south and west had been involved in ethnic conflict.[236]

[234] Sheridan, G. (2011). How I lost faith in multiculturalism, *The Australian*. Sydney, News Limited, http://www.theaustralian.com.au/national-affairs/how-i-lost-faith-in-multiculturalism/story-fn59niix-1226031793805

[235] NSW Police to form elite anti-gangs unit. *SBS News*, 25 June 2017. https://www.sbs.com.au/news/nsw-police-to-form-elite-anti-gangs-unit, accessed 16.6.2021.

Bashan (2013). Asian crime super squad to have first money-laundering taskforce, *The Daily Telegraph*, 30 Nov. https://www.dailytelegraph.com.au/news/nsw/asian-crime-super-squad-to-have-first-moneylaundering-taskforce/news-story/881369bb08ff1efaf5654bfb361a3941, accessed 16.6.2021.

Ugur Nedim and Zeb Holmes (2017). Middle Eastern Organised Crime Squad to shut down as police target "silent crimes", 10 Oct. https://www.sydneycriminallawyers.com.au/blog/middle-eastern-organised-crime-squad-to-shut-down-as-police-target-silent-crimes/, accessed 16 June 2021.

236 Patty, A. (2008). White flight leaves system segregated by race. *The Sydney Morning Herald*. Sydney, Fairfax, 10 March,

By 2016 "White flight" from ethnically diverse schools had become common in cities and rural areas, driven partly by perceived risk to the children.[237]

Earlier, on 11 December 2005, a race riot occurred in Sydney, a rarity in modern Australia. In preceding months, gangs of young men of Muslim Lebanese descent laid claim to Cronulla Beach, where they harassed Anglo beach goers. The harassment included sexual taunting of young women. The resulting climate of fear culminated in the assault and hospitalisation of two volunteer surf life savers, both belonging to the local Anglo community. A protest organised in support of the life savers grew to 5,000, but lacked marshals and the discipline of experienced demonstrators. About 150 young mainly Anglo men became intoxicated and began assaulting individuals of Middle Eastern appearance. The ethnically motivated riot incited violent reactions by groups of young Muslim Lebanese men, who caused extensive property damage and injuries in several Sydney locations. The reprisals included attacks on individuals selected for their Anglo appearance.

In overview, this was an ethnic conflict initiated by Lebanese Muslim youths attempting to claim Cronulla Beach as their territory. The conflict might be

---

http://www.smh.com.au/articles/2008/03/09/1204998283744.html, accessed 25 June 2016.

[237] Jacks, T. (2016). White flight: Race segregation in Melbourne state schools. *The Age*. Melbourne, Fairfax, 2 May, http://www.theage.com.au/victoria/white-flight-race-segregation-in-melbourne-state-schools-20160430-goj516.html, accessed 2.5.2016.

interpreted as motivated not by ethnic hatred but by competition for resources, in this case a desirable seaside public area. Whatever the original motive, the conflict became mainly ethnic as reaction and escalation occurred. In one incident, a church in Auburn was burnt down. The church was not frequented by Anglos but, as noted earlier in section 7, Christianity is the traditional western religion, and religion often serves as an ethnic marker. In another incident, a Lebanese Muslim pulled down an Australian flag from a Returned Services League (RSL) building, urinated on it and finally burnt it. Both the flag and the RSL are Anglo symbols. Attacks on random individuals of Anglo appearance, including a stabbing, also occurred. Those were not acts of resource competition but ethnic hatred.

The mainstream media alleged that the conflict was initiated by racist Anglos, and largely played down the initiating role played by Lebanese Muslims. Arguably this reporting was also Anglophobic.[238]

---

[238] Noble, G., Ed. (2009). *Lines in the sand : The Cronulla riots, multiculturalism and national belonging.* Sydney, Institute of Criminology Press.

Clancy, G. (2006). *The conspiracies of multiculturalism: The betrayal that divided Australia.* Sydney, Sunda Publications, pp. 6-28.

For an Anglophobic retrospective on the Cronulla riot, see: "'All it took was a trigger': the racism of the Cronulla riots, 15 years on", *SBS News*, 10.12.2020. https://www.sbs.com.au/news/all-it-took-was-a-trigger-the-racism-of-the-cronulla-riots-15-years-on, accessed 12.7.2021.

Commercial motivation was involved in another case of Anglophobic violence. In 1977 Donald Mackay, a community leader in the Riverina, was murdered at the behest of the local Italian Mafia. His body was never found. Mackay had been disrupting the crime syndicate's lucrative drug dealings. Although the killers' primary motive was financial, the Mafia leaders who ordered the murder were organised along ethnic lines separate from Anglo-Celtic Australia.

The public was outraged by Mackay's murder. A royal commission established under Philip Woodward QC. An attempt was then made to deflect attention from the killers by Al Grassby, an ex-politician from the Riverina. Grassby had been a long-term critic of Anglo Australia. He had been immigration minister in the Whitlam Labor government and race relations commissioner under Malcolm Fraser. His successful activism had earned him the title, "father of multiculturalism". Grassby circulated a document that accused Mackay's wife and son of his murder.[239] For many years Grassby had been receiving financial contributions from the Mafia family identified by the Nagel Royal Commission as responsible for Mackay's killing. Bruce Provost, a senior investigator with the National Crime Authority, claimed that Robert Trimbole, who had ordered the killing of Mackay, paid Grassby $40,000 to circulate the document.[240] Thus anti-Anglo sentiment was a facilitating factor among

---

[239] Sheehan, *Among the Barbarians*, pp. 135-138.
[240] Small, C. and T. Gilling (2009). *Smack express: How organised crime got hooked on drugs*, Allen & Unwin (Kindle edition 2010), p. 13.

those who ordered the murder of Donald Mackay and in the attempted cover-up.

There is further evidence pointing towards the criminal origins of Australian multiculturalism. An important element of the multicultural system is the suppression of Anglo identity by an array of organisations, both corporate and governmental. The most important legislative basis for that suppression, the Racial Discrimination Act 1975, was introduced by Lionel Murphy, federal attorney general and a member of the left faction of the Whitlam Labor government. That legislation mandated the ironically-named Human Rights Commission. The terminology and ideology were imported from the United Nations.[241] As noted earlier, the Commission has often been headed by minority activists or radicals with axes to grind against Anglo Australia.

The evidence is overwhelming that Murphy, like Grassby, was corrupt and had criminal associates. Murphy died of natural causes before being tried. But multiple witnesses attested to his criminal conduct, including police who overheard his telephone conversations and a judge, Clarrie Briese, who described first-hand Murphy's attempt to pervert the

---

[241] UN International Convention on the Elimination of All Forms of Racial Discrimination, 1965.
https://www.ohchr.org/EN/ProfessionalInterest/Pages/CERD.aspx, accessed 2 August 2021.

Lopez (2000) *The origins of multiculturalism*, p. 272, describes the RDA's reliance on the UN, and notes that the Act, "more than any other piece of the Government's legislation, had the greatest potential to establish the legal framework for a multicultural society".

course of justice.[242] A commission of three retired judges was appointed by the federal parliament to consider the many allegations made against Murphy. Fifteen allegations were "drawn", that is, found to be within the terms of reference and backed by sufficient evidence to warrant trial. Fourteen of these were served on Murphy before the investigation was wound up due to his medical condition.[243] The second of these allegations was that Murphy improperly colluded with Morgan Ryan, an organised crime figure accused of arranging illegal immigration of Korean and Filipino prostitutes.[244]

It is reasonable to conclude that two of the most influential architects of Anglophobic multiculturalism were corrupt and involved with organised crime. Grassby's associates were involved with illicit drugs

[242] Dennis Shanahan (2021). No longer a silent witness, *The Australian*, 5 March, https://www.theaustralian.com.au/inquirer/clarrie-briese-no-longer-a-silent-witness-in-the-neville-wran-corruption-scandal/news-story/58724c35271920db46ae2e429448bc53, accessed 10.3.2021.

[243] Parliamentary Commission of Inquiry (1986). Allegations drawn and served [on Justice Lionel K. Murphy, 19 August, http://dl.aph.gov.au/C63%20-%20Allegations%20drawn%20and%20served.pdf, accessed 2.8.2021.
(2017). The Murphy files. *The Australian*. 15 September, pp. 1, 6-9.

[244] Parliamentary Commission of Inquiry – Parliament of Australia, Documents received from [police], http://dl.aph.gov.au/C15%20-%20Allegation%20No.%202.pdf, accessed 5 October 2022.

and murder, Murphy's with illegally bringing women and girls from poor Asian nations into Australia and then profiting by exploiting them as sex workers. Multiculturalism has always been about immigration. The immigration of poor people into a rich country means a transfer of wealth which can be exploited by ruthless actors. Murphy's introduction of multiculturalism legalised what had been illegal wealth redistribution. This led to rich pickings for immigration lawyers, educational institutions and their enablers in the political establishment. The multicultural system that Murphy and Grassby helped to impose on Australia was an especially dangerous component of the cultural revolution that swept the West in the 1960s and 1970s. The moral corruption of these two players was such that they felt no compunction in hijacking the Commonwealth and steering its coercive powers against the people that created it.

It is important to note that although individuals of criminal character helped impose multiculturalism, it is also true that many advocates of that ideology, from the beginning until today, have been well intentioned. Shortcomings due to naivety or confused social analysis do not make them dishonourable. This is not to suggest that they have been without fault. Few, if any, have been sufficiently free of ideological blinders to dissociate themselves from immoral individuals on their side. Although they are no longer praising Grassby and Murphy and other Anglophobes, they have never admitted that multiculturalism is a vehicle that has been driven recklessly by dishonourable as well as honourable individuals. Neither have they explained how Anglophobic multicultural policies differ in practical terms from their own. Multiculturalism's taint of criminality is symbolised by the life-sized bronze statue of Al Grassby that stands to this day in the Multicultural Centre in Civic, Canberra.[245]

One of the consequences of multiculturalism has been the importation of substantial numbers of Africans, many of whom were settled in Melbourne, Victoria. Violent crime by African youths in Melbourne has been at a high level for several years as was predicted by Professor Andrew Fraser. Data from Victoria's Crime Statistics Agency show that in Victoria in 2016-2017 Sudanese-born Victorians committed violent crimes at many times the average for that state. These include serious assaults at 22 times, aggravated burglaries at 129 times, and sexual assault at 17 times the rate of the native-born population. Crime by the Kenyan-born was also overrepresented, at 15 times and 53 times the Australian-born rates of serious assault and aggravated burglary, respectively.[246] (Data on

[245] https://monumentaustralia.org.au/themes/people/government---federal/display/90108-al-grassby, accessed 21.11.2022. Also see: Sheehan, P. (2009). Monuments to honesty and deceit. *The Sydney Morning Herald*: 16 February, http://www.smh.com.au/federal-politics/monuments-to-honesty-and-deceit-20090215-881s.html, accessed 8 June 2016.

[246] Ryan, B. and G. Stayner. (2018). African gangs in Melbourne are a problem, police admit, as Victorian Government defends strategy, *ABC News*, 2 January, https://www.abc.net.au/news/2018-01-02/street-gangs-are-a-problem-in-melbourne-police-admit/9297984, accessed 14 July 2021. Sudanese-born residents committed 3 percent of the

Kenyan-born sexual assault not available.) This is not proof of uniquely Anglophobic motivation. Indeed, a senior Victorian detective reports that African criminals target Asians, including Indian students, as well as Anglo women.[247] Clearly these perpetrators have callous attitudes towards a number of ethnic groups, including Anglos.

One of the most comprehensive studies of ethnicity and crime in the USA up to 2016 broke down crime statistics wherever possible by the race or ethnicity of perpetrators and victims.[248] The study found that inter-ethnic crime is overwhelmingly perpetrated by non-whites towards whites. This suggests that "white flight" is defensive in the US, as it is in Australia.

In the UK thousands of young Anglo schoolgirls in Rotherham and other locations were targeted and

---

serious assaults committed by the Australian-born, 18 percent of the native-borns' aggravated burglaries (residents are in their house when the burglar enters), and 2.4 percent of native-borns' sexual offences. At that time, those born in Sudan were 0.1 percent of the Victorian population, Kenyans about half that. The Australian-born population in 2016 was about 71.6 percent of Victorian residents, making the Sudanese-born population 0.14 percent of the native-born population, and Kenyan-born about 0.07 percent. For the demographics of Australian-born Victorians, see "Discover Victoria's diverse population".
https://www.vic.gov.au/discover-victorias-diverse-population, accessed 14.7.2021.

[247] Personal communication, 14 July 2021.

[248] Rubinstein, E. S. (2016). *The color of crime. Race, crime, and justice in America*. Oakton, Virginia, New Century Foundation. https://www.amren.com/the-color-of-crime/, accessed 28.2.2021,

suffered sexual assault largely at the hands of Muslim Pakistani men.[249] In all these cases Anglos, a relatively individualist group, were victimised by comparatively collectivist and xenophobic minorities. These crimes have been ignored, covered up, or trivialised by the media and bureaucracy.

Whilst aggression by a white person against non-whites is often labelled a "hate crime," aggression directed in the opposite direction is rarely referred to as such and is often minimised or not reported at all by the police or mainstream media, as discovered by some victims of the grooming gangs.[250] This selective condemnation of white violence is evident on social media. Facebook, recently renamed Meta, is a giant global social media network. It is careful to censor individuals with whom it disagrees ideologically. The same is true of Google and of YouTube, owned by Google. Large numbers of content providers and internet users have been marginalised, demonetised or suspended by Facebook, Google, and YouTube, often it seems on the advice of Anglophobic organisations such as the Anti-Defamation League.[251]

---

[249] Child grooming gangs in the UK: Home Office "whitewashes" report. *EUtoday.net*, 20 December. https://eutoday.net/news/politics/2020/grooming-gangs-uk-cover-up, accessed 4.5.2021.

[250] Hill, E. (2021). "Open letter: Grooming gang survivor accuses UK government of institutional racism", 19 April. https://www.lotuseaters.com/open-letter-grooming-gang-survivor-accuses-uk-government-of-systemic-racism-19-04-21, accessed 19.4.2021.

[251] Anti-Defamation League (2017). Facebook, Google, Microsoft, Twitter, and ADL announce lab to engineer new

Facebook (Meta) provides guidance to users about which ideologies it considers unacceptable. As of 25 January 2022, its list of banned ideologies reads like an Anglopbobic wish list, so distorted by hate that it is incapable of conceiving violent ideologies that are not expressly white.

The following is taken from Facebook's policies on prohibited ideologies.

> [W]e also recognise that there are certain ideologies and beliefs that are inherently tied to violence and attempts to organise people around calls for violence or exclusion of others based on their protected characteristics. In these cases, we designate the ideology itself and remove content that supports this ideology from our platform. These ideologies include:
> - Nazism
> - White supremacy
> - White nationalism
> - White separatism[252]

These are the only ideologies mentioned. Black Lives Matter is not mentioned in this list. Neither is Marxism/Leninism, Antifa, the New Black Panther

---

solutions to stop cyberhate, ADL, 10 October, https://www.adl.org/news/press-releases/facebook-google-microsoft-twitter-and-adl-announce-lab-to-engineer-new?mod=722, accessed 19.2.2022. Google owns YouTube.

[252] Facebook (Meta) (2022). Facebook community standards – Dangerous individuals and organisations – Hateful ideologies, https://transparency.fb.com/en-gb/policies/community-standards/dangerous-individuals-organizations/, accessed 25.1.2022.

Party, or any other radical or violent non-white or anti-white movement.

Let us end this section with the caveat that not all Anglophobia is unjustified. Vilification, discrimination, and violence directed at Anglos are based on universal human potentialities from which Anglos themselves are not exempt. It follows that not all physical attacks on, or vilification of, Anglos have been unjustified.

Once it is acknowledged that Anglos, like all humans, are capable of committing ethnic aggression, it is unreasonable to describe responses to such aggression as necessarily immoral. An obvious example is times of open warfare.

It is unreasonable to accuse enemy soldiers and civilians of having had Anglophobic attitudes during wars in which their countries were bombed and invaded by an Anglosphere nation. Once war is declared and casualties occur, "bad blood" arises spontaneously. Also, hatred is deliberately induced by propagandists.

It is therefore misleading to accuse Aboriginals, for example, of behaving immorally in resisting the European occupation of their land during the colonial period, though as mentioned earlier, the killing of non-combatants on any side – men, women and children – can never be excused. The same caveat holds in the reverse direction, when Anglos defend against attackers. This is the tragedy of warfare, that it can bring good people into conflict and hate.

10. Conclusion

Anglophobia is typical of ethnic hatreds. It uses mendacious accusations that are commonly hurled in ethnic conflict around the world, such as that Anglos conspire, cheat and oppress. Anglos are also subjected to unique group defamations such as the accusation of "white supremacy". The abuse goes from vilification to casual discrimination to official discrimination and sometimes to rape and other forms of violence, up to and including murder. The most harmful Anglophobia is top-down, from academics, journalists, and senior public servants onto citizens and school children. This hate comes from the radical left as well as from ethnic bigots.

Anglophobia is real and it harms all Australians because it undermines social cohesion and injects enmity into public affairs. In particular, it is harmful to the interests of the Anglo majority who founded and built Australia and remain the irreplaceable magnet powering national cohesion. It is every bit as harmful as the other "phobias" and "isms" which are claimed to be among the worst aspects of western society. Unlike the other phobias, however, Anglophobia is practised widely, including in officialdom, without censure. It destroys trust and decays reason in public discourse. Both of these values are vital to the operation of an open and free society. Instead of trust and reason, children are indoctrinated at school to repudiate their history and apologise for it. It was not always this way; it need not continue thus.

Prior to the 1970s, Australia was widely recognised as one of the best places in the world to live. Its citizens enjoyed a high standard of living compared to the rest of the world. They also had a government responsive to the needs of the majority, through a functioning democratic system. The majority wanted Australia to remain a predominantly Anglo-European society, and immigration law reflected that preference. Governments of all persuasions did their best to protect the population from threats both inside and outside the borders.

All citizens, whatever their background, religious persuasion or ethnicity, enjoyed rights and protections unheard of in most other societies throughout history. They were afforded rights to free speech, to vote and to peaceful protest. They enjoyed equal treatment under the law and a justice system which was amongst the fairest in the world. Their elites practised the same religion and identified with the same nation, its folkways and history, which they understood stretched back to ancient times in the Old World.

By the 1970s the founding nation was being made into a pariah. It was excluded from multicultural politics while being stigmatised in the media and schools as the source of all ethnic ills. Without ever allowing a vote on these important issues, the political class imposed discriminatory policies of affirmative action and unrepresentative immigration. The advent of the internet brought some years of free speech, but censorship has since been re-imposed. Anglo – and only Anglo – advocates are ethnically cleansed from social media titans, as they long have been from the mainstream media, education and the senior public service. If anything, multicultural censorship of the internet has worsened the segregation, stigmatisation, and persecution of Anglos.

The decline of Australia's open, fair society is rarely discussed in the mainstream media, especially the ABC, and never in schools. Neither are the criminal origins of Anglophobic multiculturalism or the hostile environment this has established for Anglos. The oppression of the majority by a privileged minority is the very definition of tyranny. Yet this has increasingly been the goal of multicultural elites since the White Australia Policy was dismantled without democratic consent. Since then, Australian history from the First Fleet until the imposition of Anglophobic multiculturalism has been demonised by our elites in a process unresponsive to open debate or justification. The cultural revolution assailing Australia has always been an elite project. It was never desired or approved by the nation.

The foregoing review may be incomplete. However, this first effort is sufficient to show that Anglophobia is not only real; it is widespread, growing and embedded in major Australian institutions. As previously mentioned, Anglo-Australians have found themselves the targets of cultural warfare. They are under demographic, economic, and psychological attack. Anglo advocates were and still are excluded from multicultural forums. They are the main target of institutional attacks on freedom of speech and association. This is unacceptable in a modern democratic society. Indeed, it should not be accepted in any society.

Anglophobia is also a process. Vilification and defamation set the scene for hostile discrimination and violence. In democratic multicultural societies such as Australia, ethnic groups can defend themselves by organising lobbies that work to reduce vilification in the public square. It would have been normal for Anglos to have done this decades ago. Their failure to do so now needs to be explained.

The most obvious cause of Anglo passivity in the face of repeated provocations is the hostility of the multicultural system which was, after all, set up to oppose Anglo identity and power. Anglos may have been vulnerable to this form of attack due to their traditionally high level of trust that government, state and federal, would protect their interests.

Another contributing cause has been the entrenchment of radicalised Anglophobic elites in institutions – universities, schools, the media, and corporations. In the United States historian Victor Davis Hanson sees the left dominance of public institutions as almost complete, though infringement of free speech is still limited by the first amendment to the US constitution.[253] In Australia and America the intensity of Anglophobic hatred has increased in brazenness and

---

[253] Hanson, V. D. and J. Fowler. (2021). All the lies and pretence, https://www.youtube.com/watch?v=-vDOvEy6c_o&t=2073s, accessed 30.6.2021, from 24 minutes.

enmity as opposing voices have been silenced and the white population has declined towards minority status.

A related causal factor seems to be the rise of what sociologist Katharine Betts calls the New Class. Some university educated inner-city professionals have a political stake in boosting the numbers and influence of minorities, whom they see as a source of votes against white bourgeois policies.[254]

Whatever the precise causes, Anglos have been prevented from organising to defend their group interests. As sociologist Eric Kaufmann points out, the transformation of Anglo societies is occurring at a time when whites are the only ethnicity not permitted to declare their identity or engage in multicultural politics. In effect, identity politics as currently practised, ethnically cleanses Anglo advocates. The process has been monopolised by minorities in concert with the Anglophobic progressive left.

The demographic transformation of societies founded by Anglos is likely to continue unless Anglos behave like other ethnicities and get organised. To do so they will need to build their own lobbies. Otherwise, they could become a harried and despised minority, a situation more dangerous than being a harried and despised majority. Asking permission or apologising are losing strategies. If Anglo lobbies exercised only a fraction of the potential provided by their people's vast numbers and resources, Anglo-Australians could reclaim their seat at the policy table.

---

[254] Betts, K. (1999). *The great divide*. Sydney, Duffy & Snellgrove.

The vilification and suppression of Anglo-Australian identity hurts society in general. The drive to defame and marginalise people of British Isles descent has contributed to the breakdown of reason in the universities and in public discourse, which is bad for society in general. The insistence on Anglo racism as the main cause of inequality is so strong that public discussion of group differences can damage a person's career. Any group's loss of free speech or freedom from employment discrimination potentially compromises those rights for everyone. The drumbeat of hatred towards the founding ethnic group undermines trust across society. It has been said that truth is the first casualty of war; and cultural warfare is no exception.

Anglophobia and anti-white racism are common to English-speaking societies around the world. They have reached dangerous levels in the United States, where whites are rapidly becoming a minority due to an indiscriminate immigration policy imposed by globalist elites. The anti-white racism being whipped up by Critical Race Theory is so manifest and such a danger to civil liberties, that one expert on race relations, Dr. Carol Swain, thinks it timely for white Americans to behave like a beleaguered minority.

> I think that white people need to learn to think and act like racial minorities because they are racial minorities in many parts of the country; in ten, fifteen years they will be a minority nation-wide. We do have a constitution and laws. [W]e need to stand with our white brothers and sisters … It seems ludicrous that people that would argue that it's wrong to do it [bullying and

shaming people] to racial and ethnic minorities think it's okay to do it to whites and they don't have empathy for white children who are being taught and told to hate themselves and their ancestors.[255]

There is evidence that attitudes towards ethnic affairs are maturing. For many decades white people have been cowed by accusations of racism whenever they ventured to defend their ethnic interests. But around the time of the Brexit vote, an opinion poll found that majorities of whites in Britain and the United States did not consider it racist for a group to defend its majority demographic position.[256]

It is not only acceptable but ethical to defend one's individual and group interests. Loving one's own people is not the same as and hating others, just as parents love their children without feeling hostility towards others. Anglos are entitled to retain their own nations as are all peoples. It is a universal and legitimate human aspiration.

Anglos are still the majority in Australia, so they still have the ability to stabilise the situation. They could prevent extreme polarisation, while keeping their homeland, a place where they belong and can be

---

[255] https://www.youtube.com/watch?v=mVTO9yWX2M4&t=567s, accessed 7.9.2021, from 8:16 minutes. The interview concerned Swain's new book:

Swain, C. M. and C. J. Schorr (2021). *Black eye for America: How critical race theory is burning down the house*, Be the People Press.

[256] Kaufmann, E. (2017). 'Racial self-interest' is not racism, *Policy Exchange*, https://policyexchange.org.uk.

themselves. A homeland where they can build the best society they can and leave it to their children, as did their forebears.

Having said that, Anglos and kindred peoples have a special responsibility to moderate their clannishness beyond protecting vital interests because they have been one of the world's most powerful peoples. Due to what sociologist Ricardo Duchesne calls the "continuous creativity" of Europe,[257] the West dominated much of the world for centuries. At the same time, it has made important contributions to culture and prosperity, for example by developing analytical philosophy, the scientific revolution, republican political institutions, the industrial revolution, and the global economy.

But now the West is in retreat. Its continuation as a distinctive and independent civilisation is in doubt. Hostile elites and long-distance transportation technology are conspiring to displace the West's demographic identity.

Anglos should acknowledge the mistakes of the past, but not pass too harsh a judgment on their ancestors before comparing their behaviour contemporaneously to the rest of the world. They should treat others with dignity and respect and understand the natural inclination of peoples to defend themselves.

---

[257] Duchesne, R. (2011). *The uniqueness of Western civilization*, Leiden/Boston, Brill.

They should also expect the same consideration in return while insisting on the right to defend their own people against Anglophobia.

11. What Next?

We hope you found this book informative. If you agree with us that Anglophobia is a real and substantial threat to the status and wellbeing of Anglos, then you may also be wondering who is the best person to do something about this?

The short answer is "you".

If everyone who reads the book puts it down and ignores it once it is finished, then the message it contains will wither and die.

If, however, those who read this book decide to take action, then the harm done by Anglophobia can finally be recognised and counteracted.

Should every reader persuade more than one other person to read this book, then its message will become widely known.

By persuading three or four to do so, you will be helping to ensure that its message spreads rapidly. The old adage is correct – to be forewarned is to be forearmed.

Here are a few ways that you could persuade others to read this book.

1) Recommend it to friends, family and colleagues.
2) Make a list of people you think may appreciate it and inform them by letter or email.

3) Buy copies to give as presents for birthdays and Christmas.
4) Share the title on your social media accounts.
5) Write reviews on Amazon or Goodreads. A good review can spark interest amongst potential readers.
6) Place one or two copies in your local library.
7) Use the term "Anglophobia" in conversation or writing and link to the book wherever possible.
8) Do these things now whilst it is still fresh in your mind. Make a list if it will help.
9) Join the British Australian Community in Australia or another organisation that advocates for Anglo rights in your country.
10) Visit Anglophobia.org to keep up to date with developments.

You may have other ways that we haven't thought of yet. We would love to hear them.

Thank you for being part of the solution.

Harry Richardson (harryyo@gmail.com)

and Frank Salter

12. Index

www.ingramcontent.com/pod-product-compliance
Lightning Source LLC
Chambersburg PA
CBHW041256040426
42334CB00028BA/3034